STOP!

Before you begin I have a question for you.

Are you coachable?

If not then put this book down it's useless to you. If you are then I hope you'll allow me to coach you to success. If so here's your first assignment as your coach. Take a selfie with your book and post it on instagram. Use the hashtag #YFYI and be sure to tag me as well @sonnyd1.0

Now let's have some fun!!

YFYI
_____
YOUR FIRST YEAR IN

YFYI

YOUR FIRST YEAR IN

the beauty industry

"How to not just survive but THRIVE in the Business of Beauty."

SONNY D

1.0 MEDIA

To my boys. Anything is possible.

CONTENTS

PREFACE

Obligation. That's the word I would use to describe how this book came to be. Actually that's the word I would use to describe how my project which I refer to as The Salon Project 1.0 or TS1.0 for short, came into existence. I feel an obligation to give back, to lend a helping hand or in this case a word to the future generations or future professionals that are beginning their journey. A journey I set out on a short 10 years ago.

This is an accumulation of the things I've learned along the way. Going from a future professional to professional to learning leader/ educator to salon owner and now coach. As one who hires future pro's and occasionally has to fire future pros I set out to create a guide book, a road map if you will, to help guide you. This is not a book of theory its a book of practice. No fluff just the facts. For some it may be a reminder, for others it may be just the pep talk you need from time to time. Hopefully above all to each it's a useful utility that will stand the test of time.

INTRODUCTION

Like all great stories of beauty this one begins with a letter from Congress? Really? No really. Two years into "the project" I received this letter, to my surprise. The real surprise I guess was that it made me realize that this was the beginning of a special journey. We had arrived. Kind of.

For me I guess you could say it was a sign that we were a legit business. Legitimacy was a very big deal for me. Business is business and I've always been pretty good at generating money. To have a real business and give back to society not just take away feels alot better though. I'm getting ahead of my self lets rewind a few years.

Buckle up!

Here We Go!

Congress of the United States
House of Representatives
Washington, D.C. 20515

Gus M. Bilirakis
Ninth District
Florida

November 9, 2011

the salon 1.0
Sonny D, Artistic Director
3980 Tampa Road, Suite 102
Oldsmar, Florida 34677

Dear Friends,

I would like to congratulate the salon 1.0 on receiving the prestigious Upper Tampa Bay Chamber of Commerce "Small Business of the Year" award. I am always pleased to see that dedication and hard work are being recognized, as it is truly deserved. Congratulations!

Thank you for all the work you've done, and I look forward to hearing about your accomplishments in the future.

Warmest regards,

Gus M. Bilirakis
Member of Congress

3

How does that happen? It seems like just yesterday, on a hot summer day in July of 2003, I was lying on the bottom bunk below Andres as an inmate at a maximum security prison in the hills of North Carolina. I guess you could say I have always been a little entrepreneurial and at an early age understood the concept of supply and demand. From selling "looseys", as they are called on the block, which are individual cigarettes, in middle school to other less legal products, I have always been attracted to generating cash. The latter being how I ended up on a 3 year "vacation" which, on that hot summer day, finally came to an end. How do you go from there to receiving a letter from congress?

Why me? Why now? As I look back at the path and the journey that I have been on, I feel that now more than ever someone needs to speak up for the future of the beauty industry. Is it timing? Is it purpose? Is it a mission or is it a vision? Maybe it is all of the above? One thing I know for sure is, it is necessary. I could have never seen the future from where I was, but looking back now is the reason why I would like to connect some of the dots for you. Maybe through some of my experiences you will see that no matter where you have been, you too can change the entire course of your life if you're open to possibilities.

Lets talk about timing. What led me to choose, out of all the destinations in North Carolina, the city of Winston Salem to begin a new life, a new journey, a new me and hopefully a new path? Not having any or family or friends anywhere in the state when I had my pre-release meeting with my counselor, I remember her vaguely saying something about Winston having about a 40% chance of return rate for new parolees and that being the lowest in the state. So I said, "So there's a 60% chance I won't end up back in here? Sounds good to me I'll take it". That was it and off to Winston they shipped me.

Next up was Sweet Potatoes, a restaurant downtown where I managed to get an interview. It was owned by two very special women Vivian and Stephanie who as part of their mission to give back was to hire convicted felons and give them another chance. When I showed up to the interview with the ambition of becoming a bartender they politely said, "We don't have that position available." I mean who was I kidding. They are going to offer a bartending position, the person closest to the register, to someone who was fresh out? So like the rest that started there with a record, I started in the back of the house as a dishwasher. I swallowed my pride and went to work. As I stayed focused and put in long hours I worked my way up to become the head bartender.

It was there that, on a beautiful fall day in October of 2004, a group of people came in for lunch. As I was taking their orders I thought these guys looked really cool. Their style, their hair, they had swag. I figured they were in a band, maybe Maroon 5. Turns out, they were actually hairstylist who happened to be in town for a hair show a couple of blocks away at the convention center. They began asking me what I was doing over the next couple of days. I basically told them they were looking at it. They told me how they could really use me as a model in their show. At this moment in time I had not cut my hair for several years and had a huge afro. After spending time in the Marines right out of high school and having a shaved head for years I guess you could say I was on an anti haircut kick. I politely turned them down saying that I know nothing about being a model and had no desire to change my hair. They continued to press.

"You'll get to come to awesome parties."
"No thanks."
"You'll get free products."
"No thanks."
"You'll be around beautiful girls."
"No thanks."
"We'll also pay you $300 a day."
"Ok what time do I need to be there?"

I got the details and off they went. This particular hair show which has taken place for years at this convention center was the last one to take place there ever. This was my year. Talk about timing.

I showed up the next morning at model call. There was a sea of people. As the stylist came in and started their process of picking models it happened in seconds. Before you knew it the room had been cut down to about thirty people. As I watched them do their prep work the buzz in the air was electric. Watching what they were doing with hair and the fun that they were having was intriguing. It was like I was in another world. My only experience when it came to hair was cutting my own which I started doing at eleven years old. My little brother shaved off my front hairline with clippers while I was sleeping and I had to fix it. I actually enjoyed doing it, so from that day forward that is how I got every haircut. I had also cut my friends hair in the neighborhood because they liked what I had done with mine.

Fast forward eight years in the Marines. A couple of guys attempted to give each other haircuts at the barracks and screwed up royally. Being the only one at the barracks I ended up fixing it for them. From that point on I became the barracks barber. Finally, fast forward a few more years to my prison intake. I was asked if I had any trade skills. I told them I could cut hair and wound up working in the prison barbershop.

So, as we start to connect the dots I think I was in exactly the right place at the right time.

What these guys were doing was a part of the beauty industry I had never seen before. I mean being dragged by my mom to the discount hair salon was definitely not an experience I enjoyed. They were having fun, being creative, and it was awesome!

As I stood on stage that weekend I had what I call a "magic moment". A magic moment is a moment in time that permanently effects the course of your life. The ring leader of the show, Robert Cromeans, stood onstage cutting hair and shared his stories with thousands of stylist in the room. He talked about coming to America with only $35 in his pocket to eventually starting a small salon in San Diego where no one wanted to work for him. He spoke of the time he was doing $25 haircuts to where he was, at this point in time, charging $350 a haircut, owning several salons, and traveling the world with his team.

As I listened two things ran through my head. One, if he is getting $350 for these haircuts, I am going to be rich. I mean the haircuts that he was doing made no sense to me, buzzing off random pieces, not cutting certain pieces, I felt bad for these poor girls. For some reason though, the crowd loved it. Being so green to what was happening I had no idea what being a platform artist meant, or the fact that he was the best in the industry.

The second thing I thought as I listened to him was that I needed to learn from him. I wanted to do exactly what he was doing. He instantly became one of my greatest mentors. I saw my future flash in front of my eyes.

I took it upon myself to become his personal stalker over the weekend. Every chance I got, whether before, after, or on breaks I would ask him questions about how he got started. I asked him what steps he took and on and on and on. Wherever he went I would go. If he went outside to smoke a cigarette I was right there smoking with him and I don't even smoke! Cough, cough! Finally at the end of the weekend, a little annoyed he said, "You seem pretty into this. Why don't you go to hair school?" I thought, "Hair school?" I asked him where I would go for that. He began to tell me that Paul Mitchell had recently gotten into the hair school business, but they did not have any locations in North Carolina. They, at the time, were only located in California, Rhode Island, and the sunshine state of Florida.

Having grown up in Connecticut I thought I could go back up there, but I was ready for a change. I wondered about the other two locations. Robert asked what I was doing for a living. I told him I was a bartender and he suggested I go to Florida and that it was full of places to work and that I would easily be able to find a job there in my line of work. At that moment that is what I decided to do and that was it. The show was over and I went to work. That night, while working at the bar, all I could think about was that conversation. Over the next couple of days I contacted the Paul Mitchell school in Orlando and found out they had a class starting in January. I went to Vivian and Stephanie and broke the news to them that in a few months I would be moving to Florida. They were a little shocked and asked how this suddenly came about. I told them about the hair show experience, meeting Robert, watching him shave girls heads, wearing a kilt, and telling me to move to Florida to go to this Paul Mitchell school. They thought it sounded a little crazy, but they supported my decision and would wish me well. I saved up my money and the countdown was on. A couple of months later I packed all my stuff in a U-Haul and headed south site unseen. All I had done up to this point was to make one phone call and get the address.

When I got to Florida I went by the school it was closed, but I looked in the window and started to picture myself there. The next day I came to the school first thing in the morning to take a tour and meet the admissions leader Jennifer. She told me the class start date and showed me around. For most of the tour I was in a daze watching the students working on hair. They were all wearing all black. There was great music playing and it reminded me of the team from the hair show.

I thought this is it. The problem, at the time, was that I had not found a place to live yet. I was living in the U-Haul, running low on cash, and had no job. I had about two weeks to fix those problems. I immediately hit the bricks and found a restaurant not far from the school in Altamonte and got a serving position.

Next, I had to figure out my living situation. I did something pretty scary. I went online. I think it was roommates.com or something like that, and set up an interview. Luckily, the girl that I met, Courtney who was standing in front of her place with her boyfriend when I walked up, turned out to be awesome. I parked the U-Haul around the corner so she did not see how desperate I was. I towed my car down to Florida, but decided to leave it parked in a parking lot near by the school because the U-Haul ran better. She asked how soon I could move in and in my head I was like, "Uhh tonight.", but said that the weekend works if it was not to soon.

I found out my best friend Justin had just moved to town for school and we hooked up over the next couple of days so we could catch up. He was like, "You are going to beauty school, is there something else you want to tell me?" I told him with certainty that I had finally found my calling. Still a little confused he said, "All right man. If that is what you want to do. Good luck." I walked into to the school for the first day and after I was greeted I was brought to the financial aid office. This was perfect because I was in desperate need of some financial aid. As I sat there and we began to go over the numbers I started to cringe. I had not even found out until that moment how much school was. I looked at the financial aid leader like she was speaking a foreign language. She was going through the numbers forward and backwards, but I was thinking no matter how you look at the numbers they are all too big. Unless we are going to start dividing, I definitely cannot afford this. At that moment a lady walked in, introduced herself to me and said, "Hey I'm Tara," then she looked at the financial aid leader and said, "Andrea I need to borrow him for a second." She took me by the arm and led me into the hall way. Next thing I knew I was in a small herd of people heading down the hallway. I remember looking at the other people in the group wearing all black and all having this kind of confused, scared look on our faces. I thought this must be the rest of the broke people. We were led into a dark room, with the lights out. As we entered the lights came on people started screaming and clapping, poppers were going off and confetti was flying through the air. I thought they must really like broke people here. This was the first day of what is called CORE. Where you begin your journey. I spent the first week in school without a contract signed having the time of my life. I got tools, mannequins, books, everything, it was great.

I thought that maybe this was a try it before you buy it program. It was not. At the end of the week I went back into financial aid and agreed to pay a huge amount each month which I definitely could not afford, but knew I had to make it work. So I signed on the dotted line and the journey began.

It was a struggle from day one. The things they were asking me to do. You have to remember, my hair experience was with short mens hair, clipper cuts. The first time I attempted a round brush blow-dry the poor girl almost had to go home with the brush in her hair. I really sucked. I thought several times about quitting. I thought I had made a huge mistake. I quit a job that I loved, spent all my money moving to Florida, and now was ready to quit school. Luckily, I had learning leaders around pushing me. They saw something in me that I did not see in myself at the time. I dug in deep and kept going.

Along the journey through school I had several magic moments. One happened during a guest artist. It was a special event, we had the co-founder and dean of the Paul Mitchell schools Winn Claybaugh there doing a presentation. During a break on my way down the hall he walked past me and I said, "Hey Winn, I just wanted to say that I'm really enjoying your presentation, thanks for being here." He said, "No thank you." He then grabbed my arm and took along look at the scars that I had from my reckless days and said, "Wow looks like you have a story. I said, "Yeah I guess you could say that." He asked, "Do you share it?" I said, "No." He replied, "Well you should people need to hear it." Then he walked off. I wondered about that brief encounter for a while. I would think, "Who wants to hear my story?" I did not realize it at the time, but sharing my story was not about me, it was about who it might effect.

Another magic moment occurred in the hallway in almost the exact same spot as before. I was headed back to class and heard a deep voice say, "Are you Sonny?" I turned around and there stood the school owner, Giulio. I ran through a checklist in my head of what I had done wrong. Was I behind in payments? Had they done a background check and wanted to kick me out? Nervously after a big gulp I said, "Yeah that's me." He began to recall a conversation he had with the his friend Kevin. Kevin was in town visiting and had spent a few minutes showing us some blowdrying techniques in class the other day. He said, "Kevin speaks highly of you, he thinks you've got potential."

"Oh, cool! Tell him thanks again. "Yeah he helped me big time the other day, I've been struggling with this blow dry thing." As I began to walk off he said, "That's not the reason I stopped you." I swallowed hard again. "Ok" The reason I stopped you is because Kevin is here to run our new school that's being built in Tampa as we speak and I'm not sure what your plans are once you finish but there's a spot over there for you." I was speechless. I said, "Wow ok, I'll keep that in mind." He said, "Ok, well keep up the good work" and I went back to class. Wow what is going on here? All I thought for the rest of the day was I have got to stay focused. I am going to make this trip through beauty school pay off.

The end of school came and not only did I take the position at the brand new Tampa school, but I also landed a stylist position at a salon that had just reinvented itself and was looking for fresh new talent. The owner, Mikel, was a master at his craft and became a great mentor of mine. He showed me what being a professional hairdresser behind the chair looks like. I worked everyday day in the salon and then worked the school every night. Having two seasoned hairdressers both Kevin and Mikel to learn from was a dream come true. It was like I had finished my bachelors and now was going for my PhD. I learned not only how to be a great stylist, but also a great educator as well. Both of them were masters at education and had been educating most of their careers all over the world. I learned about salon ownership, work ethic and commitment to the craft. The experiences I took away were priceless.

Like every journey, there came a time, another magic moment when I realized there was a new mission to undertake. As the school grew from 6 students to 150 I started to hear the graduates stories about what they were experiencing as they went out into the industry. There was definitely a problem. I believe about every 10 years, the world as we know it, experiences these paradigm shifts. A paradigm shift is a fundamental change in the way things are done. With the rise of the Paul Mitchell schools, as well as others, the training and education that the beauty school student is receiving has drastically changed. The problem is that the salons of today have not changed with them. They are still operating under the old beliefs that beauty school could not possibly come close to preparing stylist for the salon. This has created a "language barrier" not to mention the fact that the majority of salon owners did not experience the beginning of their journey at one of these new schools. I just do not think they know what to do with todays graduates. After thinking about this problem for almost a year and wondering where will all these graduates go? Who is gonna be able to guide them? I decided to stop waiting for someone to appear and set out to become that someone.

In October of 2009, I opened my first salon. Actually it was my third attempt at opening a salon that year. The first two I attempted to partner with people who did not see the vision and after I had invested time, energy, and my money in remodeling and purchasing tons of products, they had a change of heart. Being a naive new business owner I never had anything in writing and was forced to just walk away, not once, but twice. That was my first real world lesson in business. I wanted to just go work for someone else. After the second time I remembered thinking that maybe this whole salon owner thing is not for me, but there was still that burning desire to help change the landscape. That and maybe I am a gluten for punishment and that pushed me to start again.

Having zero money at this point, my car being repossessed and being evicted from my apartment. I had nothing else to lose. I decided to pawn a white gold necklace at a We Buy Gold shop and I got $600, which would be my seed money. I found a turn-key barbershop on craigslist that had gone out of business. I set up a meeting and walked in with only one thought in mind, I need to make this happen. At first, the owner was looking for $30,000 cash and I could have everything. That would be perfect, except for the fact that I was homeless and only had $600. I decided to share my business plan and vision for what I wanted to do anyway. I stood there explaining the problem in detail and how by letting me take over the space he would not just be helping me but he would be helping the future of the beauty industry. I was so into my presentation I did not even notice the smile on his face. As I looked up, I stopped in mid sentence and asked him what he was smiling about.

He said, "Wow, you are really serious about this." I replied, "Yes I am. This is my career. This is my mission in life." He said, "Ok well here is what I can do. If you can come up with a small deposit we can make a deal." I said, "Done." In my head I was committed. Commit first, figure it out later. I then borrowed and begged from everyone I knew and came up with the deposit. We moved in that week, changed some paint, hung a few shelves, and The Salon Project 1.0 Inc. was born, again.

It has been an incredible ride so far. We now have three locations throughout the Tampa Bay area and there is no end in sight. There are over 100 Paul Mitchell schools throughout the country and we are going to have 1.0 salons by all of them. We are going to change lives. In the short time we have been in existence we have done over 2 million in revenue, but better than that we have stylist doing 90k plus dollars a year in revenue in just 2-3 years out of school! I think we have found our way. There is still a long way to go ,but we have our eyes set on the future, which brings us to this project. Knowing the position that I found myself in coming out of beauty school I must say that I was extremely fortunate. What about the average student that is graduating today though? Are they going to land in such a predicament? Probably not, but as I think about those graduates I decided I wanted to create a tool, a resource to lend a helping hand. Kind of like a GPS to help that person along the way. To help YOU as you begin your journey. The hardest part of the journey is that first 12-18 months when you find yourself out in the real world as a new professional. How do you get the momentum going? How do you find the right salon? What are the things that matter most in the beginning? How do you strengthen your mindset when doubt creeps in and you want to quit? Trust me it will happen. What are the realities of just starting out? What should you expect? These and more are the questions I aim to answer with this book. Let me be your personal guide. I commend you for picking up this book and hope you cannot put it down. Here is to you and an amazing journey filled with many Magic Moments!

CHAPTER 1

"I am always doing things I can't do, that's how I get to do them. " ~ Pablo Picasso

Why...Is this industry for you?

Why? That is the question. I want to start with why. Out of all the industries and occupations out there, why the beauty industry? You need to ask yourself that question. You need to ask yourself that question over and over, at least twenty-one times, and if you cannot come up with twenty-one answers then you might need to reconsider. If your 'why' is strong enough, if your 'why' is anchored in something that truly moves you, then that will give you the ability to deal with any obstacles that come your way, anytime anywhere. So, you need to ask yourself, why?

Why this industry? Why this book? If you are looking for another "How to Become a Six Figure Stylist" book, then just stop reading because this is not it. The reality is, the majority of beauty school graduates are not going to make it past their first year, let alone their first 100 thousand dollars. What is going to make you different? It is going to be your 'why'. When I think about my own 'why' I think about my two sons. That is what gets me going everyday. That is what keeps me moving forward through all the obstacles, all the adversity, all of the nay sayers, and any other challenges that come.

So I need you to think about why. What is your why? You could have chosen any industry that you wanted, you chose the beauty industry. If you are in school right now you chose to go to that school you are in. If you finished school, if you are already in the field, and you just picked up this book, then maybe you are deciding that now is your time, but you need to know your 'why'. You have to look at your 'why' like an anchor, and that anchor, just like an anchor on a ship, is going to dig into the floor of the ocean so deep and hold that ship still no matter what kind of current rocks it. That needs to be your 'why'. So, maybe for you it is your family. Maybe it is your kids. For me, I never want my kids to experience what I experienced at 15 years old, being homeless and living on the streets.

I am dedicated to never having that be apart of their story, but what about for you? That is the first thing you need to think about.

When you think about your 'why' what is it going to do? It is going to do a lot of essential things for you. It is going to hold you accountable. When you think about accountability, your why is who you are accountable to or who you are accountable for. It is also going to help eliminate some of the things I see preventing so many people from moving forward or achieving their goals. The why eliminates excuses. When you have a stomach ache and you do not feel like getting out of bed, your 'why' will cure that stomach ache. Your 'why' will remind you, why it is you're commuting an hour and a half one way to get to wherever you are going. Your 'why' is a constant reminder. You need to think about what your 'why' is and you need to write it down. If you have a picture of it, you need to keep that picture with you, because the days are going to come when you are ready to quit and that is natural. When those days come your why is what is going to prevent that. Now I do not want you to get romantic and start talking about things like, "I want it really bad. I want to make a lot of money. I want this or I want that" because all of that is just lip service. I am talking about a real reason. A real reason is something that you want, like a breath of air.

Think about the story of the teacher and the pupil. The pupil comes to the teacher and says. "I really want to learn about success and how to become successful?" The teacher says, "If you really want to learn, meet me down at the beach tomorrow morning at 6am and I will teach you." The pupil shows up and the teacher says to the pupil, "Are you ready?". The teacher takes the pupil by the hand and walks out into the water, "Is this really going to teach me what success is?". The teacher says, "Yes. You have to trust me." They begin to walk into that water chest deep. The pupil looks a bit scared and confused. The teacher does not look at the pupil at all. The teacher just has his eyes set on the horizon. They keep walking until their feet are barely on the ground. He takes the pupil and has him face in the opposite direction. The teacher pushes the pupil down under the water. As the pupil starts to flail and gasp and try to regain his head above the water, the teacher continues to push the pupil under the water. The pupil is flailing and flailing losing all kinds of balance and the teacher starts to drag the pupil, who is out of energy and choking on the water, out of the ocean. As they get to the shore and the pupil is on his knees, coughing and breathing heavily, he asks, "What are you doing! I wanted you to teach me about success and you are trying to kill me!". The teacher responds, "When you were out there and I forced you under the water, what did you think about?

What did you want? What were you fighting for?". The pupil says, "The only thing I wanted was a breath of fresh air". The teacher replied, "Well, that is the definition of success. When you want it as bad as you want that breath of fresh air, that is what it is."

So, as you are thinking about what your 'why' is, you have make sure to attach yourself to it. You have to attach and anchor it so deep, that you want it as bad as you want to breath. You will fail, but the key is, when you fail or fall is that you try to fail forward. You have to be extremely hungry because this is a long journey. Going to school and getting to the end, that final clock out, you get your final hours, it is a big celebration. Think about the celebration. The celebration at the end of the official hours is really a celebration of the beginning. It is the beginning of your career, not the end of your journey. It is just the start.

I want you think about what your why is and I want you to be thinking about how deep you can anchor it. Is it something you are willing to fight for? It should be, because this is your career. After you finish beauty school, the prep work, the start of your foundation, has been laid. The work that comes after is the real work. There are a few things that you will need to consider when you are thinking about your 'why'. As you are going into the industry, what it is that you are trying to get out of this industry?

What is it that you are trying to satisfy? What needs do you have? You will want to get out of this industry some of the basic needs, some of the basic needs that every human being has. As you come out, you want to think about needs like certainty. When you come into the industry you are most likely looking to avoid pain and you are looking for uncertainty because you want some variety and excitement. You also want to feel significant, you want to matter. You will look for connection, to be loved, as well as growth. The last need, of course, is to contribute to society and to the business that you are going to work for. These are all needs that you will want met.

One of the hardest things you will be facing is yourself in the mirror and being 100% honest with where you are at in life. When you look yourself in the mirror and ask yourself "Why am I doing this?". You must be able to make eye contact and with 100% conviction say to yourself, "This is my reason why". Whatever that reason is, it needs to be written down. You need to be staring at it, reading it, and reminding yourself of it everyday.

One of the other key ingredients in anchoring your 'why' is going to be your self image. How do you see yourself, not only from the outside in, but from the inside out? How you see yourself will be reflecting in many different ways. How do you dress up?

Are you dressing up for the job that you have or are you dressing up for the job that you want? When you think about the potential earnings, what your goal income is, whether it be six, seven or eight figures, it doesn't start when you get to that level. Your image starts now. So you need to start dressing up before you ever get to that level.

Another key ingredient is going to be your confidence. Now where does that confidence come from? Well, a lot of it does not come naturally. When I was coming into the beauty industry I was very excited and had a lot of enthusiasm, but I definitely did not have much confidence in what I was doing. I did not feel prepared to deal with any situations that I was going to be faced with in a real salon environment. I had my education to back me up, but I no longer had my teachers there to check my work. I was now independent, not co-dependent. So where does that confidence from? It is going to come from practice, knowledge, and a constant never ending goal to improve your skill set every single day.

For me, a lot of what strengthens the confidence, is something that in our company is called brain aerobics. I want you to try to imagine what the human brain looks like. The massive tissue inside your head between your two ears. A lot of times when it comes to our brains, it is one of the most neglected parts when it comes to our anatomy. You can see people spending time on their biceps, triceps, legs, all different muscle groups, in the gym relentlessly trying to improve their outside appearance while neglecting the mind. Their mind has not seen a gym in forever. Their mind is out of shape, unconditioned and an utter mess. Why is that? What can you do to change that? Well, I believe it begins with a healthy diet. I would recommend to start with, at least 30 minutes a day, of some sort of positive programming. That may be an audio program, reading 15 minutes, or 30 minutes of positive information in a book, such as this one or other books that exist. There are other resources that you can use, like youtube or Ted Talks. I will share some of my mentors that I listen to and read from in future chapters. In this day and age there is no shortage of information. Thirty minutes would be my recommendation. Since I have started this, mind aerobics for 30 minutes a day is non negotiable, and it has completely changed my outlook. It keeps things in perspective. It keeps your focus and further cements your 'why' and the reason you are doing what you are doing.

One of the other things you need to be, if you are going to make this happen, is you need to be sold. You need to be completely sold and convicted on the mission. "I am going to make it through this first year!". You need to develop a mentality, that I call a "burn the ships" mentally. This is from one of the ancient voyagers, Cortez, who landed on an island with his crew and ship. When they landed they knew they were grossly out numbered. Cortez instructed his crew to burn the ships. That's right, light a fire to the only means of transportation they had from the island. He said, "We will either conquer the land and defeat the enemy or we will perish. That is the only option." When you have a 'why' that is that strong and you develop a "burn the ships" mentality, you gain a key ingredient, resilience. If you are going to make it through this first year you must develop a "burn the ships" mentality. You will need to have the hunger and develop the resilience and it is going to come from your 'why'.

So I want you to start thinking about and ask yourself the question, "Why am I in the this industry? Why do I need to not quit? Why is my success imperative?". Ask yourself those three questions and write down the answers. That is going to give you clarity and make you resilient. It will keep you focused on the goal and task at hand. You MUST know your 'why'.

CHAPTER 2

"Do not go where the path may lead, go instead where there is no path and leave a trail." ~ Ralph Waldo Emerson

Resumes, Portfolios, and Other Wastes of Time

Now, now, now, I know what you are thinking. All that time you spent on that resume, the expensive 30lb stock paper that you got it printed on, with that fancy texture, just the right shade of off white, the font that you selected, the marginal indents and spacing and time you put into it, how could it be a waste? Before you throw it out I want you to think about this, I am speaking to you now as a salon owner. I did the same exact thing. I prepared this beautiful resume, not too much not too little. I followed all of the instructions of the best resume classes and recommendations that I could find on google and for what? Here is what I want you to think about, what is a resume?

A resume is history. A resume is his or her story, but either way it is a past reflection. It is a past tense and has no barring on the future. I want you to imagine with me for a second, what if you were to present a resume in the form of the future focus? So, if you are reading this now, whatever date is on the calendar, for example say it is November 28th, 2015 and this is your first year, and your mission is to get a job. When you go into meet Mr. or Mrs. salon owner and you present them with this beautifully crafted resume, from talking to other salon owners and being a salon owner for the past 5 years, I will tell you this, most of the time no one is reading your resume. They may look at it briefly and read the objective which seems to be the classic same opening line on a resume. They will note your name and email and use it as a reference to call you or not to call you. Other than that there are very few parts that a business owner can use because it's all about what you did. When you get hired at a salon it's not about what you did but about what you are going to do. So here in this chapter I am going to propose that we get rid of the resume. That we redesign the portfolio and stop wasting time on giving a past experience or giving a backward look, and start thinking about this as a forward look. If I were to be a first year beauty professional, coming into this industry, going back looking at what I know now from my experiences in interviewing and seeing resumes, I would approach it totally different. I would start with this, the future. Think about this, if you began to forecast based on your experiences up to this point what you would do in the future. I want you to think about where you are at. What is your current status? Maybe you have just graduated and have worked on some guests in school or maybe you are going into a new job and have already worked on guests in the salon. What if you were to start to forecast what your goals are? What if you start to forecast how many guests you would have in the first month, in the first week? What if you began to forecast and write a resume of your forward looking projections of where you are going, not where you have been?

Now, I know this may sound strange and you really have to stretch your imagination, but what makes your past resume different from anyone else? I have seen many resumes as a salon owner and I can pretty much tell you this, besides the font, the texture of the paper or the shade of the paper, they all follow the same exact format. When you come into this industry with your goal of landing your ideal job, at that ideal salon, what is going to make you any different? What is going to separate you from the rest of the pack? This could be one of those things. This is also a visionary idea so some of you might be thinking where to begin? Well, lets start with this, you have technology at your disposal. Nowadays you have the ability look up the salon that you want to work at. Hopefully they will have a website that will list pricing and stylists and may have a career path. Start by looking at the pricing structure and where you could potentially enter their career path. Where would you start in the pricing model? From there, what would you do? You want to start to chart out what your first thirty, sixty and ninety day goal objectives would be. For example, say you notice that the beginning hair cut for a new stylist was $25. You projected, in the first week that you were there, that you would have at least three guests a day. You saw those three guests and you knew that their cut was $25 and their color was $50. That is $75 a day and maybe if you added a unit of retail to their ticket, thats a potential score of $85 per guest. So, what if you started to project an average ticket of $85? How many guests would you see a day, how many would you see a week? What would your projection be for your first month, for you second month, for your third month? What if you started to project, just as business would do? Whether a new business owner is going in to either win a new contract or obtain financing from a bank, they bring in a business plan. It's forecasting. So, I want you to start thinking about yourself as a small business. That is how you will create separation from you and every other resume out there. You have to understand there is a possibility that the salon will move forward with you. Therefore they will want to know what kind of person they are dealing with. Do they have a visionary? Do they have someone that can see the future, think about what is to come, and that has foresight and goals? Or do they have someone that is living their future riding the highs of yesterday? So it is a forward looking resume. Try that exercise.

I want you to think about that salon you want to work at. I want you to do some research and find out what that salons pricing structure is. Take the data and create what an average ticket would be what an average dollar per guest would be. Think about how many guests you will have your first day, your first month, second month, third month and start to project and write down. You can use the past data as a starting point. You know where you have been, but for a salon that's looking to hire somebody for the future you need to be able to paint a picture for that salon owner of not the past but, where you are going. That is how you become an asset to a salon. Now, lets discuss the portfolio. A portfolio is a great way to display your work, a great way to display your achievements but, again it is backward glance. As you start to design a portfolio, I want you to think about what hair is going to look like in the future. Think about what trends are coming up. Some of that may be difficult to display because you may not have the work, but start to think about what the ideas would be. Many times we do these in an idea book and we put down ideas that we want to do, but we never necessarily project that through images. So think about how you, a future stylist of that company, can start to portray what the trends are going to be, what direction hair is going to move in, what the direction of art is going to be. What are some ideas that you can present that will get the owner excited? I can tell you this, as a salon owner, most of the time we are thinking about what direction the company is moving in. So be able to position yourself to bring in futuristic ideas of what you can do with hair. What you can turn hair into. Even if it is in your portfolio and are things you have not done on a person, but things you have just tried on a mannequin. These ideas will show the salon owner your vision of the salon in the future. Future is where it is at. If you can present a resume and portfolio that are forward looking, I promise, you will stand out. I know in the 5 years as a salon owner or even while in school, I have never seen anything like it or even heard the suggestion. As I was thinking about this topic and I was looking at all the resumes I collected, they all looked the same. What is going to separate you? What is going to make you different?

So begin on creating a forward looking resume. Start looking at a forward portfolio and working on what your business is going to be like 30, 60, and 90 days after you start. What your artistic expressions are going to be like in the 30, 60, and 90 days? If you can start to arrange this, it will not matter what style paper you are using or what the font looks like. The information will be the key element. That is what the future looks like. Some of the information will be on paper, some will be digital presentations of the future of what you are going to do. So, you my friend, yes you reading this book right now, this is the beginning of turning yourself into an asset. The companies of today, every company I can think of, their number one goal is to create more assets and reduce liabilities. By you showing this forward looking, visionary, approach you will definitely stand out above anyone they have ever interviewed.

CHAPTER 3

"Sometimes the heart sees what is invisible to the eye." ~ H. Jackson Brown, Jr.

Salon InterviewS- It's not love at first sight

Yup, you got it right, this is a chapter on interviews. InterviewS with a capital S. When are you going to start? What are you going say? Where do you go? What do you do? Many people think it is love at first sight and I am here to tell you it is definitely not. Getting hired at the first salon you interview is kind of like marrying the first person you date. You would never think about doing such a thing, it is ludicrous. Well, it is the same with salon interviews. I know when I was in school I was thinking about salon interviews and I was hearing about salon interviews, but the problem was I was not doing salon interviews. If you already finished school and you are reading this and you have not done any interviews, then you are behind the ball. If you are in school and you are reading this, start interviewing right away. Now, I know what you are thinking. What do you mean start right away? I have no experience, I have no idea what I am doing, I just started school for crying out loud. My recommendation remains the same, start right away. The sooner you start the sooner you can qualify or disqualify different suiters. It is like dating. You are going to date probably more than one person before you find the one. As you are going on these dates or interviews I want to give you some key questions and tips that will make your salon interviews a success.

I know you have all these great questions in your head, have heard about good questions to ask, and have probably googled questions to ask. The challenge for most is having these questions written down. Again, I have done a great deal of interviews in my time and I did not notice that being the case in most interview scenarios. When people show up, sometimes they are empty handed with no notebook, let alone having any questions written down. You will most likely think about questions that you have on your way home from the interview. They are going to hit you on your way as you are driving away or walking out the door and it is going to be too late. So have your questions and make sure you write them down. I would recommend at least five questions. You may have to force yourself to ask them. I am going to give you some of the key ones. Actually these are some of the ones that I never hear, which I am pretty surprised by. Now as you are looking at these questions you can start to formulate your own, but these are some of the key ones you are going to want to know when you are interviewing. I want you to know it is a two way street. Not only is the salon interviewing you, you are interviewing the salon. You should be interviewing the salon to see what kind of suiters they may be, because I am sure there are things you have in mind that you want and of things that you do not want. Just like dating, you have questions in mind and you have things that you will not tolerate. Sometimes we end up in relationships and before we know it we are in way too deep dealing with things we would never put up with. Since we never wrote it down and it was never made clear by asking questions in the first place, we struggle to figure out who takes what, who keeps the dog and so on and so on. When you go into an interview here are some of the key questions you should ask.

1. Continuing Education - This seems to be a hot topic. What is the schedule of the continuing education and how often does the salon train? I have heard stories and have had stylist tell me the salon they are interested in has continuing education, but what does that look like? Does that mean once a week, once a month, once a year? You want to know the schedule? So what is the schedule for continuing education at your salon?

2. Career Path - What does your career path look like? Meaning, what are my opportunities for promotions? What are the different levels and requirements for a promotion? What can you be expected to receive from a promotion? These are great questions to ask because sometimes a salon will make things up on the fly. I'm sorry, but I know that a lot of salons that are opened by frustrated, former stylist who have not decided to commit to any form of career path or systems and now all of a sudden are hiring. I know If I am a stylist going into a salon, I not only want the answers to these questions, but I also want to see everything in writing. Now, is it too forward for you to ask to have these answers in writing, I don't think so. I actually think if you are in the right scenario and you are interviewing the right salon owner they would be more than forthcoming to show you an example. Whether it be in an operations manual or some other form. The key is that it is written somewhere you can see it and see it exists. Once you start it is very hard to stop and regain this ground

3. Pay - I cannot tell you how many times I have been in an interview and the subject of pay never comes up. Now, I am not saying you are going to understand everything about pay, and we will talk about the ways to get paid in the upcoming chapters, but at least knowing what are the starting points. How do we get paid? When do we get paid?

What do we get paid for? These are things you definitely want to ask. You are not going to want to wait until you get home and you are super excited because you think you got the job and then your mom says, " Oh thats great! How much are you getting paid?". Oh you have no clue. So it is okay to ask in an interview how much you will be getting paid.

A couple other key points when you are going to an interview will involve what you're going to wear. You have to remember you only get one chance to make a first impression. So you want to dress to impress. That should be your attitude everywhere you go as a beauty industry professional. You would be surprised how many people show up in faded clothes, unkempt hair, no makeup and just not looking the part. When you show up to an interview you want to make sure you are wearing and looking your best. You want to make sure your hair is done, there is no room for error. Your wardrobe, your makeup, down to your shoes, everything must look great. That will be the lasting impression which will be the first impression you make on the person that is interviewing you.

Another key point is arrival. You want to arrive early. If the interview is scheduled to start at 2:00 you want to be at least 15 minutes early, maybe 30 minutes. Anything beyond that may be a little bit excessive. If you arrive 15 minutes early, that speaks volumes to the person interviewing you. It shows that you are serious about employment, and that your career means a lot to you. Now what if you arrive to the salon and there is no one there? That is okay, but the fact that you are there will stand out. So make sure you arrive early, give yourself enough time, make sure you have enough gas, and know the directions. If it is somewhere foreign or you are new to the area I would also recommend you drive the route the day before so you know exactly where you are going so there are no slip ups in the morning. I always like to think about building 15 minutes of "just in case time" on the day of the interview.

The next important key is staying late. Just because the interview is scheduled for thirty minutes let the interviewer tell you, the interviewee, when it is time to go. They will have a way whether, it is through body language or wrapping it up with a statement like, "All right, we are all set" or something to that affect to let you know it is time to go. You want to stay as long as possible. Many times, during the formality part of the interview and all of the Q&A is done, some of the actual other information that happens post interview is just as valuable. It is just as important as the interview itself. So when possible stay late.

Another thing to remember during an interview is to take notes. Going back to arriving empty handed, not a good look. Show up with a notebook, a pen that works, and take notes diligently on everything that is being said. You can write your questions down. This is a great way to present your questions. Take notes, whether big or small points, make sure you are taking notes and documenting. It shows that you are serious, committed, you are willing to learn from the person interviewing you.

The next key is something that I notice often with new generational workers, new beauty industry professionals going in, young or old. I notice this being a very big void. The void that I am speaking of is the ability to follow up, not just follow-up, but follow-up persistently. One of my mentors has always said that the fortune is in the follow-up. There are a few key things that I like to think about when it comes to following up. When you are following up with somebody, the first rule of thumb is that you continue to follow up until someone dies! Thats right, dies! I can think of stylists in my organization that would not be apart of my organization had it not been for their persistence in following up. I am talking about following up to the point where I almost wanted to get a restraining order on them! That is how much they followed up. They did not wait around until I got back to them. Lets talk about that. So you decided there is a salon that you are interested in. You send them an email. You send them an email one time and you do not hear back from them, not in a day, not within a week and you get offended. "Well, they didn't email me back, they must not be interested" you say to yourself. Here is my recommendation on that. If you are attracted to a company that is growing and you email either the decision maker, or the owner, who ever that person may be, hopefully if they are growing they are extremely busy. So do not take that as a sign of them not wanting to talk to you or not being interested in you. I said that this is 'like' dating, but not dating. This is not a sign that they do not want to talk to you so definitely do not take it personal. Take it as they are extremely busy. Maybe they are working on growing their company. Maybe they are fielding a lot of different inquiries. You need to keep on following up with them. This has worked for me in any endeavor I have faced. I will never take it personally and I will follow up with email after email after email. Could it get annoying? Yes, it could, but do I stop following up until I hear a reply? No, I don't. How much is too much? Until someone dies. So that is something you need to commit too. Following up. One of the other parts about following up is that you have to be frequent. That frequency is what is going to trigger them to think about you. You need to stand out. Sending them one email a day is not too much. I had someone send me an email every single day for a week and now that person in one of the top money earners in the company. In the beginning was I little annoyed. Yes, I wish she would have left me alone, but who do you think I thought of when we were short staffed? It was that person. It was the only person, because they had gotten in front of me so many times I immediately thought of them. The last part of following up is to be creative. You want to find different ways to get in front of them, whether you are using social media, sharing a picture, tagging them in a post or sending an email or letter. Your mission is to follow-up until someone dies.

The last part that I will share, when it comes to salon interviews, is verifying what you hear. You need to be able to understand what you are taking notes on. So, what I am going to recommend is to repeat back what you hear. If it is a question about career path, training or education and they tell you we train once a month," and you repeat back to them "So, you train once a month? Is that correct?". Then they confirm that or they say, "No, we train every other month." You want to make sure that you are repeat back what you are hearing. You want to confirm and verify what you hear. That is a skill that is sorely missing in salon interviews.

Finally, when it comes to interviews, remember it is not love at first sight. Start early, interview often, and by doing so, you will find the salon that you truly want to begin your career at.

CHAPTER 4

"Keep score, you do more." ~ Robert Cromeans

Chapter 4
Show Me the Money
Numbers Don't Lie

This is where we get into the nitty gritty, hacking the "business of beauty", or what I like to call 'hacking the bob'. When we begin to talk about numbers, many times people start to cringe. For the most part, things that are measurable, weight, age, money and numbers, become uncomfortable for many people to talk about. At the end of the day we need to remember that this is a business. Unless you decided to go to beauty school to start a non-profit salon, one of the things you decided is that you want to earn a living. So where will you be if you do not know the numbers. One of my rules of thumb for every stylist that I work with, every salon owner, and every future professional, is to know thy numbers. That is the deal. When you think about numbers there is a reason why most people do not like them. The reason is because they are not that good, not the person, the numbers. If your score sucks you are not going to want to look at it very often, but no matter where you are you have to start somewhere. Trust me, my first set of numbers when I started in the salon where bad. I had zero clients so I had a bunch of goose eggs. I think the first year I was in the salon we may have gotten one walk-in. That one walk-in, of course, came to me and it was a start. A lot of what happens with numbers is that we make up excuses. Like "Oh I am not good at math," or, "I don't get it". These are all excuses we make up, but when it comes to money we are constantly complaining. We never have enough money, we are struggling, we are trying to make ends meet. So my recommendation in this chapter is to make a commitment to yourself, to your family, to the business that you work in, and remember your 'why'. Know your numbers. It is a do or die.

So, lets take a look at numbers. Let's start with "break even", your first reality. You went to beauty school and now you are coming out into your first year. When I was coming out of beauty school I could only think of a few things that sounded logical to me. I heard of this term in the financial industry and I wanted to make sure I understood it completely and that term is 'breaking even'. It means getting back what you put in. I do not know what your tuition is or how much you have invested over the course of time you were in beauty school, but I want you to start there. I want you to think about breaking even. Your first year you want to survive, but you do not want to JUST survive, you want to thrive. I do not want you to come out of beauty school thinking you are going to make six figures in your first year. Now could this happen? Yes. Has that happened? Probably. Has it happen to me or my stylists? No. I am going to share with you actual profiles of stylists and exactly what played out. This was not in their first year either. This was in their second going into their third year.

Lets break down 'break even'. Say with your expenses and all you paid $15,000 to go through beauty school. Maybe on top of that $15,000 you had another $10,000 of other expenses. That would put you in a range of $20-$25,000 dollars spent in that year of school. Not separating your tuition out from your other expenses, that would be the total that it cost you for that time.

So, your first year in your beauty industry, thinking realistically, let's set a goal of breaking even. That is a reasonable goal. You are coming out of school with zero clientele. Maybe for some of you, you will have your mom. Hopefully she will follow you and not continue to go to school or like most expect you to do their hair at home. So say she does follow you, you will have one client. You are starting at ground zero. You will have to build up your reputation, your experience and your demand. You will not come out of school with any of these therefore you will have no money or no income. You are going to have to start somewhere. As I was coming out of school and into my first position in the salon I had no idea of what to expect. There are many different resources you can look and see what the average income is, but I am going to tell you, from reality and having coached and trained new stylist in their first year, break even is a good starting point. At least earning what it cost you your first year in beauty school. So you need to figure out what that number is and make it your target.

As you move into that first year I want you to think about one of the scary subjects that nobody likes to talk about, "What do I get paid?". Now there are few different scenarios that can happen when you come out of school and into the salon. I will cover them both. The first scenario you may come into is hourly. I will tackle this first, because it is easy and pretty cut and dry, no pun intended. Hourly means you are getting paid a wage for an hour or unit of work. This could be negotiable. Whatever the business owner says you can negotiate higher. They could say, "No this is firm" and it could go back and forth, but that could be negotiable. The number of hours you get is going to be dependent on what that business needs. So say they offer you $9 an hour at 30 hours a week, that is a "gross" pay of $270 before taxes. The "net" is what you take home, so understand those two terms. The gross, as it was explained to me by one of my mentors, is the ocean and the net is what you will cast into the ocean to catch some fish. Whatever you pull out, meaning what you take home, is the net. So the difference between gross and net is a term that I want you to understand when it comes to finances and the numbers. That is pretty much hourly. Now you are capped at hourly and how many hours you can work. The salon owner will determine that and handle all of the back work, i.e. taxes and everything on the back end of your pay and when you will receive your pay for the hours worked.

Now moving into the world of commission. When we talk about commission, that is a hot topic in the world of hair. Someone way back when came up with one specific kind of commission structure that I will share with you shortly. Then as time went by we started to see all different structures, different percentages, charge backs, fees for this, fees for that. It can become very confusing to the point when an average stylists gets their pay check really has no idea how they are getting paid, where they are getting paid and what they have to do to get paid more. So I want to uncover some of those mysteries and unlock the labyrinth of pay when it comes to commission. Starting with one of the myths that you need to know, the percentage. Many people get hung up on percentage. It has nothing to do with how much money you take home when it comes to big picture thinking. Here is what I want you to think about. Say you were to come in and I was to woo you and offer you 70 percent commission if you worked at my salon. That sounds great as a lip service, but the reality is that if you come in and you just finished school and this is your first year in the beauty industry, you are going to get a big whopping 70% of nothing. So 70% of zero, my friends, if you are following along with the math, still equals zero. Why do I want to share that with you, because one of the tactics used to appeal new stylists is the higher commission percentages being offered. New stylists hear 70 , they hear 60, and think, "Wow this is a great deal!". Keep in mind, you maybe have one client, being your mother. The other thing, I want you to think about, is when you are looking at percentages, there is the percentage of service and also the percentage of retail. These are separate numbers we are going to look at those each independently. Now way back when someone decided to come up with a commission structure, for lack of creativity and lack of looking at the economics of business, as a fifty-fifty split. What I want you to ask yourself, as a first year stylist coming into the industry is, "What am I taking 50% of and what am I getting 50% for?". Those two questions alone will help to answer a lot of questions. For example, in some salons you may get 50% of the service commission that you do, but for that 50% what is the salon providing? That is going to be something that you want to know. Are they providing all of the tools you will need to complete the job? Are they providing the color, the electric tools, the towels and everything else that you would possibly need inside the salon? Are they are providing any frills and any extra added benefits for the salon guests that you are able to take advantage of? You want to know all of these answers, because at the end of the day everything that you are responsible for is going to be an expense that you are going to incur.

The next thing you want to know when it comes to what the salon is providing is that you want to know the retail. Is there commission on the retail you sell? Typically, what you will see in many scenarios, is the salon offering you a 10% commission on the sales that you make when it comes to retail. For example, if you sell $100 of retail you would get $10 on those retail sales. I use these numbers because, not only are they round and easy, but they are also very common in many scenarios. What I have discovered along the way is that many salons, when they begin this process and start with the traditional scale of commission, they realize that at the end of the day they do not have enough money to stay afloat. So they introduce to the salon and stylists what became a term called a 'charge back'. You want to know whether there is going to be a flat rate commission or if there will be a charge back for use of tools and product. This is a perfectly fine question to ask. If there is a charge back for things like color, treatments, and for other uses of items you are going to want to know, because those charge backs will be discounted off the original commission of the services and possibly the retail. These are things you want to be made aware of and remembering at the end of the day when you are getting paid as a commission stylist you want to have a transparent view through how the commission is structured. My warnings to any new stylists coming out is, if it sounds too good to be true then it probably is and you are going to want to look at the math closely.

When you are thinking about commission and thinking about hourly, you will probably wonder which one is better and which one is worse. Honestly, starting out as a new stylist, having zero business and zero clientele, the answer is going to depend on you. Are you self motivated? If you are self motivated then a commission structure would be ideal, because there is truly no limits. It will depend on your motivation, your hard work and your dedication. If you do a lot you will make a lot. If you do nothing you will get nothing. It is truly based on performance, versus an hourly pay where you do have that security net that is built in. You know as long as you are new and building your business you do have some income coming in while being paid hourly. Some salons actually offer both options. That is going to be something that you are going to want to find out when coming into a new salon and definitely a question that should come up in an interview. The other option that I want you to think about is your own space. Maybe you will rent a space, a suite or a chair at a salon. The cut and dry of that scenario is this. You need to understand two line items, profit and loss. If you have more coming in then your expense going out then you are in what we call the black. If you have more going out then coming in you are in what we call the red and that is not a good place to be. I would not recommend having your own space unless you truly conducted yourself and positioned yourself in a scenario where you know you can cover, not only your expenses, but obtain a profit. Once again, this is a for profit business you are in business to make a profit. Now, when you think about going into a salon and you are looking at a pay structure, knowing the opportunities that exist, is going to be something you want to obtain a great amount of information on. Where are you starting and where are you going? Remember, seeing this on paper is a fact. Hearing about it from the owner is just fiction. Knowing what the pricing structure is, are you going to be able to move up the pricing structure, is it set by the owner, do you select your own prices? These are some of the questions I would raise when it comes to the money.

The other thing I want you to think about when it comes to the numbers is, which numbers should you be paying attention to. There are five key performance indicators, or as I call them KPIs, that I want you to know before you begin your journey, before you first year. These are numbers that you should pay attention to even while you are still in school. So what are these KPIs, or key performance indicators? They are as follows.

1. **The Average Ticket**. The average ticket is the service and retail divided by the number of guests you have. For example, if you do $1000 in service and retail and you have ten guests then that average ticket for service and retail would be $100.

2. **The Average Service Units per Guest**. How many units of service did every guest get? If you have 10 guests and they all got hair cut and hair color thats an average of 2 services per guest.

3. **The Average Retail Units per Guest**. Did every guest buy a bottle of retail? If so, that would give you an average of one unit of retail per guest.

4. **The Average New Guest per Month**. How many new guests are you averaging per month?

5. **Rebooking Percentage**. What percentage of guests rebooked before they left the salon?

Now wait, there is a bonus KPI and that is the frequency of visits or as we call it F.O.V. How often are your guest coming to see you? You want to measure this on an annual basis. I am going to give you some averages. These are just averages we measure against and when I am talking about averages I am talking about minimum thresholds, good bench marks that you can use when you are looking at the beauty industry and where your numbers could be. So, when it comes to frequency of visit, we know from the data that frequency of visit for the industry, since 2008 has slipped quite a bit. Before 2008, the financial crisis, and everyone being put into a financial bind, the frequency of visit was 8 to 10 visits a year. If you can imagine your guest coming to see you every 6 weeks that would be an average 8.67 visits per year. Why has this slipped so much, because people, once they became financially strapped, they were looking for ways to extend the life of their visit to maybe not visit every six weeks, but maybe going to nine weeks or even longer in some cases. Looking at six weeks as a starting point, a good number to be shooting for would be eight visits per year. Rebooking percentage, based on industry averages, you want to try to aim for something in the realm of 70 to 80 percent or higher. Average new guest per month is something we look at, at a weekly basis. So think about having at least one new guest per day. You cannot have less than one guest per day because we cannot cut people in half. So I look at that number and I determine that by how many days a week I work. If I work five days a week, I am looking at five new guests a week, times 4 weeks a month, that would be 20 new guests a month.

When it comes to units of retail that is another number where the lowest possible number you want is a one. Data shows that the industry average right now for guests taking home retail is less than one bottle per guest. I do not know how they are doing that, but maybe they are taking home a squirt in their hand or sample packs, but I think a realistic number for guests is one unit of retail.

Then there are service units. Service units are tricky. One of the examples I want to give you is banks. When you think about banks they lure you in with a great sales pitch. The way you are hooked into a bank is by them offering the infamous "free checking" account, but as you know nothing is for free. What happens is, you open up a checking account and then the bank immediately offers you maybe, a savings account on top of that, then maybe an investment account or a car loan or a mortgage and business loan if you get to that point. The goal of the bank is to offer you the most services, because the more services you are enjoying and using from that bank, the more likely you are going to be a customer for life. Same thing applies when it comes to the salon. The more service units your guests experiences beyond the one service the more likely you are able to retain them. So as an average we shoot for 1.5 services as a minimum per guest. Some of the top performers in the industry average 2 to 2.5 services per guest.

The average ticket really comes down to what your main two services are. Now, in the salon you will find the main two services are probably going to be cut and color. So start with that, if you have ten guests and every other guest receive cut and color you are at least looking at the haircut price plus the color price divided in half. When I start to think about service plus retail you have to look at the average dollar amount per retail item. When you add those two numbers together that is how you will be able to come up with your average ticket. It will depend on the salon that you are in or on the salon you want to be apart of to determine what your average ticket is going to be. I will share with you this, on average, right now from data that we receive, the average service ticket overall is around $40-$45 in our industry. We are experiencing a higher average ticket in our salon and I am going to share with you some stylist profiles to show you some real data.

Lets talk about getting a raise. Now that you have an idea of what numbers you want to pay attention to, how you are getting paid, what your immediate goal could be coming out of beauty school, how do you progress, how do you move up? Getting a raise is one of those things we think is sometimes a given and it is not a given, it is earned. When we think about getting a raise, getting a raise does not just come, it is not an annual review, it is not a pat on the back or a sign that someone signals an owner and says, "It is time for so and so to get a raise". How does a raise come? A raise comes by creating value. In every organization there will be opportunities for you to create value for the organization, meaning finding additional streams of revenue. Your mission to get a raise is to find where additional streams of income live. Whether it be, you increasing the amount of services a guests has, increasing the amount of guest you have, or increasing the amount each guests spends. Those are going to be the three key ways you can get a raise. So you need to look at creating value and you need to have quarterly talks or one on ones with the decision maker or with the owner on ways you can create more value. As you are working with the salon, having that open dialog is going to be key. Understanding those numbers, as well as, knowing what you need to do in order to get to the next bench mark is also key. Remember, when you are talking to the owner, you want to have an open conversation, open knowledge, and the access to know what kind of information the owner is looking at to critique you on when it comes to earning a raise or making more money. A true business owner, which you are becoming by coming into the beauty industry, is going to be very aware of the numbers. Know thy numbers or die. I want you to think about it like brushing your teeth. It is something that needs to be done daily, not just done weekly, monthly or quarterly, but daily. You may have a formal one on one with the owner or manager, which is great, but unless it is daily, a lot of the work is up to you to know how to access the numbers. You do not get a pass on this one and there is no excuse.

There are a couple more things I want you to think about. I want you to think about the lifetime value of a guest. Not a one time value of a guest. Many times I watch new stylist come into the industry and they try to hit a home run on every single guest. In order to build a career that is going to last you want to build a lifetime value. You want to build value in the guest. The guests of today are coming in today for simple things. If you can take care of maintenance and you can see them on a regular repeat basis that is how you are going to build a long lasting profitable income stream that is recurring. In our business recurring revenue is the lifeblood. If you are not able to provide those services in a reasonable time, for a reasonable amount of money, on consistent basis you will not have a chance to build value of a guest. Those guest then turn into referring guests and they refer people that are looking for the same consistency. So I want you to think about lifetime value in terms of 4-5 years. If you have a guest, for example, that is coming in, and they have an average ticket of lets say $60. That $60 that they are spending is going to be something consistent that they do every six weeks. When you take the 52 weeks that are in a year and divide that by 6 that leaves you with 8.6 visits. When you multiply 8.6 visits by $60 a visit that equals $520 dollars. When you look at that over the coarse of 4 years that brings you to $2080. Now here is the question, if you knew that a guest walking in, for their first time, was worth $2080, how would you treat them? The only way you will realize that amount of revenue is to look at the guest as lifetime value and not a one hit wonder. This is a big mistake that I see a lot of new stylist make. They try to go too far, just like dating. They go too far on the first date and never see the second date. So think about lifetime value and put it into perspective. When your guest comes in they are looking for simple things so remember the acronym, K-I-S-S. Keep It Simple Stupid. Meaning, not trying to go over the top because you just watched a dvd or just got back from a hair show and you come back trying to perform a hair show on a guest. You will overwhelm them. With time, trust, practice and patience you will be able to try plenty of your newest techniques and you will have plenty of guests that, once they have the confidence and trust in you, will sit down and say, "You know what? Do whatever you want". Until then, I want you to keep it simple stupid.

Lastly, we are going to talk about R-E-D. How do you know when you are ready to receive a raise? You have been looking at your KPI's, you are tracking your numbers, and meeting with your owner. R-E-D is going to be the final determining factor, reputation, experience and demand. These are things that we look at on a regular basis. When I have a stylist that is booked 80 to 90% of the time, no one can get in with them, and they're meeting all the minimal averages when we look at our key performance indicators, that tells me that they are in the RED. They have the reputation, they have the experience, and they have the demand. These are some of the big factors.

Numbers do not lie, so if you are looking to be promoted or you are looking to promote yourself, if you are working independently, you want to be able to look at the KPI's and if you are in the RED it is time to move up. That is when you know. You owe it to yourself, you owe it to the industry, and you owe it to the other stylist that are watching you, to set an example. You must set the bar higher and keep raising the bar. So remember, the numbers don't lie. You can look at the case studies at the end of the book, for what a 2-5 year stylist is capable of doing. It's just as an example for you to see, but this is real data and real numbers that we look at. These are the key KPI's that I want you to focus on. Whatever kind of system you are using to gather this information, even if you do not have a system, you can still do the basic math formulas that we talked about and figure out what your KPI's are. I cannot tell you enough, numbers do not lie. When you look at numbers as foot prints you will know where you are and where you are going. This will be key in building a solid business and not just surviving, but thriving.

CHAPTER 5

"Winners never quit and quitters never win." ~ Vince Lombardi

Hustle muscle
What's your DNA?

Today we are talking about different names of generations. You hear the words going around, generation x, generation y, now we are talking about the millennials and I have even heard the term generation flux. There is also generation W-A-S, as in weak ass sauce. What happened? Where did the hustle go? Hustle is something that cannot be denied. Success acknowledges one thing and one thing only and that is hard work or as I would like to say, hustle. To be able to build this business and to get what you want to get out of this business you are going to need to exercise this muscle. Now how do you know if you have the hustle muscle? You are rising before everyone else, you are arriving early, you are staying late. These are the signals. One of my mentors says that you need to have an immigrant mentality. When you think about it, when an immigrant comes to our country what do they have that you do not have? What do they have that you need to develop? One of the things they have is that they come to this country with the mentality of looking for freedom, taking care of their family and they are dying to get here. If you were lucky enough like I was to be born here we need to take some lessons from immigrants. Statistics show that immigrants are three times more likely to become millionaires than America are. The interesting thing I find is that only 13% of our population are immigrants and when it comes to millionaires there are only 1 out of 25 families that are millionaires so what do they have that we don't? They have what I believe is called the hustle muscle and that starts with an attitude. It is an attitude that is going to get you to work through the pain. Developing this hustle muscle does not take a lot, it just takes a will. Saying to yourself things like, "I will do this" and not giving yourself an easy way out. As I look at the generation that is coming out, the new producers, the generation that is coming into the work force, the highest producing generation that the world has ever seen, I do believe there is a lack of hustle muscle. I believe we are growing up in a generation of softness, a generation of entitlement, a generation of, "I showed up, that should be enough, now pay me." Now that is not going to work, especially in our industry. Our industry is huge. It is a 54 billion dollar industry, but the competition is fierce. There are hair salons and opportunities for people to get these services almost on every corner. The person that shows up early, stays late and has the hustle muscle is guaranteed to win. One of my mentors said the only place success comes before work is in the dictionary and I believe that this true. What would it mean to you to work through the pain? I think back to days when I woke up in extreme amounts of pain, when I was in the military, and still had to suit up and show up to perform. Calling in sick was not an option, but in todays day and age that one act alone is costing the workforce billions of dollars.

What is it going to take to develop your hustle muscle? Well, when you think back to the "why" that will be a part of it. When I talk about generation W-A-S or weak as sauce. What happened? Is it because we were given a trophy even though we finished last in a competition? Nowadays everyone wins, but the reality is everybody does not win. Life is really good for a lot of people, kind of ok for the majority, and not good for the rest. The reality of America and the American dream is still alive and well. I believe it exists. I do not believe there is any opportunity on the planet better than that in the United States of America. The only problem is Americans not realizing it and thinking it is beneath them to hustle. Hustle is what this country is built on and will be a key ingredient you will need to survive your in you first year.

Here are some of the things I want you to think about when it comes to hustling. Building your business is a 24 hour operation. You do not get days off whether its Sunday or Monday, our typical two days off in our industry. Every time you leave your house you have the opportunity to come in contact with someone. So you need to have the mentality that business is everywhere. The products and services that you offer as a beauty industry professional can be found anywhere, but most of the time people are not ready to offer them therefor they are missing opportunities. Just like we talked about your 'why' and wanting success as bad as you want to breath, you have to want to build your business in the same mentality. Just when you think you have done enough you have to dig deeper, you have to tell yourself one more rep and then I will stop. For most of us this muscle that I am speaking of was referred to as work ethic. Working 50, 60, 70 hours a week amongst high net worth individuals is common practice. You look at some of the highest net worth individuals in the world, people like Warren Buffet, at 80 plus years old, still works every single day. There is a reason why he is in the position that he is. It is because of work ethic or as I refers to as hustle muscle. In the generation that we are in now, because we maybe are in a cycle where our parents were the hustle muscle generation, that we have now decided to take a back seat and ride on their hard work. For you as an independent business owner, which I need you to get into the mindset of being, you need to develop your hustle muscle. You need to be thinking about a few things. You need to think about, what do you need to do and if you do not do it who is going to suffer? Starting with myself, my family, my friends, and of course my 'why'. Our hustle muscle has gotten out of shape over the last few years. We have gotten accustomed to having things now, having things quickly, getting things in a hurry, not having to work for it and just having things happen for us. There has been too much of that and this hustle muscle has gotten extremely flabby and out of shape.

So how do you know? I want you to think about clock punchers. Many people live and die by the 9 to 5. One thing I will share with you is, any person that is earning six figures or more on average is working 60 hours a week. Your first year is the most important year. This is your do or die year, where there is an 80% attrition rate, this will be a deciding factor. How much time will you dedicate to building your business. If you are a spring chicken and you are just getting started why not put the extra time in now so you can reap the benefits later?

Remember that what you are building is an asset of recurring revenue and if you build it right once you will not have to build it again. When I look at the current generation and I look at the lack of muscle and the lack of hustle it is kind of scary. Scary because I know that the generation that is coming up now is not going to become the generation that we are hoping it will be. We are looking at this generation as doomed. They have not learned some of the basic principles of success, hard work, dedication, and persistence. I do not want to bore you with the, "When I was your age I walked 16 miles in the snow to do a haircut" speech, but you do need to compare and contrast. Nowadays there is a lot of life work balance talk and that seems to be cool on a lot of the forums and blogs on the internet, but what does work life balance mean? For some it means they are not understanding what is work and what is life and how to balance it. If you are committed to your career then your work and life truly can co-exist. If work becomes a burden and you are looking forward to just getting through the week, then you will never get from the week. When you truly find the career that you love and that you enjoy then work and life are co-mingled.

Being in the beauty industry is one of those careers. I cannot imagine doing anything else. Being around beauty professionals, being able to work with people that I enjoy working with, being able to give to people the confidence they get when they receive our services and use our products, when they feel more confident when they leave the salon then when they entered, truly is priceless. Understanding that building a clientele still requires an extreme amount of dedication and in the beginning when you have no reputation and you are not in demand is when you need to turn it on and turn it on high. Freedom is not granted. You do not get to show up and then just get the reward and benefits. The older generations and the older work force talk about "paying your dues". I do not necessarily agree with paying your dues, but I do believe working your face off to get what you are due. You may not be the smartest, the prettiest, the tallest, or be the sharpest when it comes to a lot of areas, but where we are all on the same level playing field is when it comes to hustle. No one has more time in a day than another. No one gets an extra day that they can squeeze in and no one when it comes to hustle has more or less given to them at birth. Hustle is something that you develop. It truly is a muscle. You need to exercise it. You need to be thinking about ways you can do what you need to do and if you do not get it done then your work continues. Too many people are ready to clock out or quit before their mission is accomplished. When you are thinking about your career and you are thinking about what is it going to take to get where you want to go you need to think about exercising your hustle muscle everyday of the week. Yes, that is seven days a week. There is no other way and there are no short cuts to freedom. If you think there is then you might not be thinking clearly about freedom. In fact you may just be free dumb.   Everything short of stealing, I'm talkng begging, borrowing, scratching, and kicking, are the things you are going to have to do to get where you want to go, to get out of the rat race.   To escape generation d or generation doomed or weak-ass- sauce is going to take dedication. Remember, success only acknowledges one thing and that is WORK. Work is hustle, dedication, and persistence. The sooner you realize that and start to develop this muscle the sooner you are on your way to building a solid business. Not one that you are going to rebuild because it was not built on a solid foundation. One of my mentors said repetition is the mother of all learning. So are you going to do it and repeat it over and over again? That is how you develop the ultimate muscle. That is how you develop the hustle muscle.

CHAPTER 6

What you "WANT" shows up in conversation. What you "EXPECT" shows up in behavior. ~ Sonny D

NETWORKING- DO OR DIE

When it comes to the topic of networking a lot of people cringe at the thought that you are going to have to go out and meet and talk to people you do not know. The fact that you are going to have to walk up to them and solicit business sometimes makes people feel like they are about to throw up. You have to understand, networking is not anything to be afraid of, it is just the way of life for a new stylist especially. It is just what we do. Although tools like Facebook, Instagram, Twitter and all the other social mediums, have made physical networking seem like a thing of the past, nothing, I repeat nothing, will change good old face-to-face networking. So when it comes to networking I want to share in this chapter some of the key things that you are going to need if you want to build your business.

Let's start with that little rectangular piece of paper. You know what I am talking about, the business card. What is the business card? For some people it is a way for them to say that they are a professional, that they own something or that they are important. At the end of the day some people just look at it as a piece of paper with your name, number and maybe some other information. What information should be on a business card? For starters your name needs to be legible and it needs to be clear. If you are making your own business cards make sure you're using a font big enough for people to see from a distance. One test that I like to do with a business card, is to throw it on the ground a couple feet away and see if I can still recognize the name and possibly a logo. Other pertinent information you are going to want to have on the card is an email address and a phone number where you can be reached, whether it is your business or your personal number. Also, something you can think about, is if you have a title, maybe a specialty or any other title that might be pertinent for someone to identify you as. Bigger than just the information on the business card, what I want to talk about is what a business card represents. When it comes to building your business, lets use the example that I used earlier in the book, in "Show Me the Money". So let's say that the average ticket of your guests is $60 and the average FOV (frequency of visit) that they were coming to see you is eight times a year. Then look at the LV (lifetime value) of a guest. How do we get that you ask? We use the $60 a ticket, times 8 visits a year and get $480. We assume the typical lifespan you can expect of a guest is 5 years, based on our data. You can always retain a guest longer, but typically it is five years. So $480 x 5 years gives us $2400. So beyond the piece of paper, beyond your name, your email address, your phone number, and any other title or logo that you want to have on your business card, each business card has a potential value of $2400. Let me ask you this, if you had a piece of paper in your hand that had a value of $2400 how would you treat it? I have seen crazy things happening with business cards over the years. I have seen people sticking them under windshield wipers, sticking them in doorjams, leaving them on some counter at some little store with 2000 other cards. They are just tossed all over the place. Is that how you treat $2400? I want you to think about making over your business card. Not so much the look, yes aesthetically it should be appealing, simple and clean by design, but more so making it over mentally. Treating it like it has the value that it does.

When you are introducing a business card to

somebody ask yourself a couple things. Number one, did they ask you for it or are you trying to force your business card down peoples throats? If that is the case, most likely, it is going to get circular filed, meaning it is going in the trash. When someone asks for your business card that is when you should introduce it. If you are at a networking event and business cards are being exchanged make sure there is a connection and make sure during the conversation, when somebody gives you their business card, hold it in your hand the entire time that they are talking to you. Holding it with two hands in front of you increases the conversations value and increases the importance you are placing on their card. You also have their business info in front of you as well as their name so you can use it in the conversation. I have been to networking events where people will just take my card stick it in their pocket and never even take a look at it, never even read it and I know nothing will come from that exchange. I just continue the small talk and move on. One time, after a minute of talking, they asked what I did. Had they practiced what I am teaching here they would not have looked like an idiot. A business card is a powerful tool, if you treat it like one. Only put your business card in the hands of the people you want to do business with. When you see somebody that you are thinking would look great in your chair then you want to create conversation and you want to open dialog with them. At the end of that encounter there may be an exchange of a business card and it will feel natural. One of the other things, when it comes to networking, is this thing called responsibility. You have a responsibility to yourself to build your business. You are not going to be relying on someone to do it for you. That is not how the real world works. How the world of business works, especially in the beauty industry, you need to be responsible for building your business. You need to make a commitment.

There is power in numbers and I am going to share a couple equations when it comes to thinking about networking and business cards. What I want you to think about is the law of averages. Everything that is measurable can be monitored and everything that you measure will get done. When it comes to looking at averages I want you to start tracking from day one how many business cards you are giving out. One easy way to do this is setting yourself a daily goal for business cards to be distributed. For example we will start with a week. Say for the week your goal is to distribute five business cards a day. This needs to be a non-negotiable. That means that when you leave the house in the morning you do not come home at night until your mission is complete. That is your mission, to distribute five business cards, to potential new customers, in their hand. What happens if you get busy? What happens if you get caught up in the grind of the day and at the end of your day you realize you have not met your quota? What happens is that by being responsible this means you do not go home until you meet your quota even if it means you have to make a couple of extra stops on the way home. Remember this is your business, this is your career, and building it is part of the process.

So, I understand that you are new at this and may be asking where do I go to build my business? I know when I was new I did not have a clue. There are many places you can go. You can start by looking up networking groups in your neighborhood. The local chamber of commerce is a great place to start. They have morning and evening meetings and most of them will be free to attend. If you like the group you can also become a member for a fee and take advantage of all the perks. When you are looking for new guest, stay around a 5 mile radius from the salon that you are working in. Even if you do not live there it is going to be the immediate area around the salon that the majority of the salon guest are going to come from. You want to start looking in that area and expand from there. Start going to new places in that area. Try new services and products at the businesses in that area because that is where the people are going to be. Do not sit around and wait like the Maytag man waiting for somebody to stumble in and end up in your chair. The other thing I do not want you to do is, expect your friends or family or whoever you think from your neighborhood, especially if you live an hour away, to travel and come and see you. It is just not going to happen. I am letting you know this now because over the years as I watch stylist, some of the ones I have had it opportunity work with, have come from out of town or have come from far away cities maybe as much as an hour and a half away. They pass out cards in their local area thinking people are going to make that trip. It is not going to happen. I need you to be thinking about your immediate area and be thinking within a 5 mile radius.

I want to share a few icebreakers with you. Depending on where you are at on how you would start a conversation with a stranger. First example lets say you are in a restaurant. Going to a restaurant is a great opportunity to meet the staff and also meet other patrons of the restaurant. The server begins by coming up to you and taking your order. But what do you do? Do you engage in conversation or do just let them take your order and walk away? I am going to suggest that you engage. Ask them questions like how long have they worked there, do they have a second job, are they in school? Asking questions is a great way to open conversation. Asking questions shows interest and disrupts peoples thought patterns. It also is usually reciprocated and that may lead into you being able to insert some information. Maybe you just came from work and let them know that or let them know that maybe you are there on a lunch break. This is going to prompt them to potentially turn around and ask you a question like, "Oh where do you work?". When they do that is when you can say you work in a salon right around the corner from there and you can let them know that you are new to the salon and that you are building your business. If they look like a potential customer then that might be an opportunity for you to give them a business card. Now notice the wording I used there, "New to the salon" or "new to the area". Your first year out of school I do not want you to lie to people, but I also do not recommend that you tell them how you just graduated last week. When you say something like that you lose the confidence of that potential person. They start thinking in their head, "I'm not going to see some rookie that just finished school". You may be awesome but they do not know that yet. The time that you were in school counts as experience the minute you started. So if you took a year or more to finish school then you already have a year or more experience. You do not want to discount that. You want to say that you are new to the area or new to the salon. The salon may have been there for years so letting them know you are new to the area does not throw up a giant red flag saying, "I'm brand-new, I have no customers and I'm desperate for business."

Another scenario, what if you are in the mall and you are shopping for clothes and the store clerk comes up to you and asks you if you need any help. The normal response is "no just looking". It is time to disrupt their thought pattern again. You could let them know that you are looking for clothes for work which may prompt them to ask what it is that you do. Then you have another opportunity to introduce what you do. See how easy this can be? Your mission in networking is to create interest when you run into potential customers. You ask questions. They ask questions back. It is pretty easy. You need to practice your lines if you are not a natural networker, do not have a gift of gab and you do not go out and socialize a lot. You are going to need to come up with what your pitch is. A pitch is just a commercial. It could be as short as 30 seconds. A pitch is something you could say to somebody in an elevator. Just to briefly introduce yourself and what it is you do. Maybe something like, "I'm hairstylist and I just started working in the area." If you have a specialty or something that you want to specialize in you could say, "I'm hairstylist I specialize in color. I'm a hairstylist I specialize in men's grooming." Whatever it is have it down. Practicing that pitch is going to be key. One of the ways that I like to do this with new stylist and even when I am working on my own pitch is by practicing in front of the camera. It is not going to come out smooth the first time so don't sweat it. If you think of any great movie or any great lines of any great movies how do you think those scenes occurred? It wasn't the actor just coming up with it on-the-fly. They practiced it and they rehearsed it and they studied their scripts so much that when they said it, it came out like it was their own. If you write your script down, read it a few times, and then record yourself reading it, you can watch it and you can see how you sound. Practicing in front of the camera is nothing new. Practicing in front of the camera is what all great performers do. Professional athletes as well. When they are in their off-season they spend the majority of their time watching game films of themselves. Watching it over and over and in slow-motion, rewinding it, fast forwarding it and watching it again. Why do they do this? They are studying their moves, studying their script. They are studying every angle so they can become great. Our profession is no different. If you want to be great you have got to practice how great people practice. So set up your camera and get rolling.

Another great way to network is by talking to your existing guests. As you start to build your business and start to have traffic coming to your chair you must never discount the person sitting in front of you. They are going to be one of your greatest resources for new business. The kind of business I love, the referral business. I would much rather prefer building a referral business than any other type. Having people seeking you out because they saw your work and are already sold on you is much easier than trying to get any other type of business. When it comes to referrals though, a lot of us are afraid to ask. We do not want to seem desperate so we finish our guest and we let them leave maybe giving them one or two business cards. This is not a formula for success. What needs to happen is that you are asking for referrals. Here is some dialog that you can try on.

You just finished up, the hair looks great and you are talking to the guests at the end of service. One of the things you can say is, "Kim would you help me out?" Now that is a great opening line because naturally people like to help people.

Kim is going to say, "Sure what is it?" When she says sure, what is it you are going to say? "Well, I'm new to the salon" or "I'm new to this area and I'm really working on building my business. I really enjoyed working with you and I want to give you three of my business cards to share with three of your friends that you'd recommend to come and enjoy the same experience that you had. Would you do that for me?" What do you think Kim is gonna say? Unless you butchered her hair and turned it green then she is going to say, "Of course."

Practice this line over and over. You may want to tweak it depending on the guest, but asking for help is a great way to ask for referrals. The other thing that you are going to want to make sure of is that you are being specific. Notice in that dialog I said three cards for 3 of your friends. You want to be specific and give them a goal.   Remember, what gets measured car be monitored. Kim will be happy to take your cards and she will be on the lookout for three friends.   The number one reason that guest do not send other people to the salon is because no one ever asked them to. Asking for business is nothing to be ashamed of. If you have ever been online lately or driven down the road you see billboards, advertisements, you see pop-ups in your Facebook newsfeed, all of these are "asks". Those businesses are asking for business and you can be no different. If the biggest brands in the world are asking for business on a regular basis then what do you think you need to do.   You also need to be tracking your referrals. Make sure that you have a method to do this so you know what is working and what guest are working for you.   Maybe the salon has an automated system that you can pull up a report and track, but regardless, track the number of referrals that you get.

The other thing that I would like you to think about is what are your referrers getting? What is in it for them? Of course there is the benefit of them helping you which is what they wanted to do in the first place, but also if there is a way that you could reward them that is a bonus. Talk with your salon owner and if they already have a reward system in place make sure you know what it is. Also, make sure that you are making the guest aware that when they refer somebody they will get rewarded. If the salon does not have one in place then as a new stylist you need to be a visionary and possibly create one. Remember referrals are one of the strongest ways to ever build your business.

Here are few other things when it comes to networking. You need to be thinking about your image and you need to be thinking about it all the time. What do we sell? We sell style. So it's important that our image is well put together. Whether it's a classic look that's timeless, a trending look representing the current trends, or a fashion forward look, you should always be constantly aware of your appearance. Have a current haircut, current hair color, and current style. From head to toe make sure your image is that of a true professional. Before you leave the house I want you to look in the mirror and when you look in the mirror ask yourself the question, "What am I selling?". Having a well put together image is also going to create a more positive feeling in yourself and people are attracted to that. Your positive self-image, because of your outer image, will draw guest to you as well, so make sure you are being aware of your image.

One of the challenges that happens when people start networking is that sometimes people think they are doing more than they actually are. If you think you are networking and you are not tracking it, you are probably not networking. You need to be aware of exactly where you are going and exactly what you are doing. If you are frequenting one place too much, you know everybody there, and you have not gotten any business yet, maybe it is time to move on. Tracking is everything. Also, the amount of action that you take matters. If you think your action is enough and you are not getting the results that you want then I am going to recommend that you double, triple or even quadruple it if necessary. Action is something that you are going to track by knowing the amount of cards you are passing out, knowing the number of places you want to target in a given week, and knowing how many referrals you want to get or have gotten. These are three indicators you are going to want to pay attention to.

Another thing I want you to think about is your approach. In the beginning you are going to get a lot of "no's" before you get to one "yes". One example of how many approaches it is going to take to be great is seen when you look at the game baseball. If a baseball player has a batting average of 300 they will be paid millions and most likely end up in the Hall of Fame. What does a 300 batting average mean? A 300 batting average means that out of 10 at-bats they strike out seven times. That is seven "no's" for just three "yes" and they are in Hall of Fame status. So for a lot of people that are networking they are just not getting enough "no's". They are not approaching enough people, not taking enough action, and so it does not seem like networking works. Trust me networking works. When I was building my business in the beginning, tracking cards, asking for referrals, and tracking everywhere that I went, the results were phenomenal. My personal best, out of 10 cards passed out, was two guests. Not quite in the Hall of Fame, but pretty good and I was on my way. I need you to be thinking about that because, in the beginning you may only be getting one out of 10 cards passed out which is a pretty reasonable starting point. With that data then you know if you want to get five guest, for example, you need to pass out 50 cards. That is right, 50. I know it seems like a lot, but it begins, what I like to call, the numbers game. In the beginning you have to make up in numbers what you lack in skill. The averages never lie and when you can spot what your average is then you can find ways to work on increasing it. There are really three main ways that you're going to focus on building your business. The first is going to be your APPROACH, working on your pitch, working on how many people you approach and how often. The second is going to be the ACTION. The amount of action that you take toward your goal everyday. The third one is going to be your ATTITUDE and if your attitude stinks so does life. You need to constantly work on it to stay ahead. You need positive input. You need to think about what and who you are surrounding yourself with. These are some of the key components. Take a personal inventory looking at your surroundings and be honest with yourself.

The last thing I want to leave you with is social media and then we are going to talk about the fast track challenge. Social media is something that I love. I am on every social network probably known to man. I enjoy going on there. I enjoy the different types of tools that are available so I definitely want you to maintain your social media presence. I also suggest you build a Facebook fan page or business page that can represent you as a business or your brand. One thing I want you to think about is that social media whether it be Facebook, Twitter, LinkedIn, Instagram, or any of the others is not, I repeat is NOT, a replacement for the one-to-one marketing and one-to-one networking approach. Sure I want you to use social media, but remember social media is just a utility, just like your business card is utility. They are both tools, but without you there is no magic.

Our business is hands-on. When you are out meeting people that will always remain to be the best way you are going to build your business. They can see your style. They can get a feel for your character and at the end of the day it is that personal attention that every one is craving. So use it as a tool but do not rely on it as an only resort or hide behind it.

Lastly, the fast track challenge. Some of you are going to want to build your business on hyper-speed. So I am gonna give you the challenge. It is pretty simple to explain, but requires serious tenacity, persistence and resilience to complete. Many have tried, fewer have succeeded. Do you have what it takes? I guess we will see. It is called the 90 day Fast Track challenge and it will explode your business. Your goal is going to be to pass out 10 cards a day. That is 10 cards to 10 people. Not dumping them on the counter somewhere and not putting two in the bowl at a restaurant, it is 10 cards, one individual at a time. That is 10 a day for ninety days and if you do this seven days a week you will build an incredible business and you will build it incredibly fast. Think about the math. On average we are talking 70 cards a week. 70 cards a week times four weeks a month, that is 280 cards every month, times three months that's 840 cards! If you look at that and you figure you are going to get about a 10% return, that is 84 guests that you should have coming your way at the end of that ninety-day Fast Track. 84 guests may not seem like a lot, but when you look at that over three months that is an enormous foundation to start with. I also want you to consider that you can earn a six figure income from really just 200 loyal guests. From there you can take advantage of the power of compounding and now you have 84 people that you can ask for referrals. 84 people to introduce to new services, and 84 walking talking advertisements out in the community. So think about the Fast Track challenge and if you are game to do it you will want to have an accountability partner so make sure you email me at sonnydts1.0@gmail.com and I will be happy to help you out by tracking your progress. Now, get out, start networking, and build your business. Your future depends on it!

CHAPTER 7

If you work hard on your job you can make a living. If you work hard on yourself you can make a fortune. ~ Jim Rohn

GOALS
Set em' but don't forget em'

This is one of my favorite topics. When I am working with any stylist or any business I always start with looking at where they are going. Goals are basically a roadmap that you are going to follow for not only your first year in the beauty industry, but your entire career. Why must you have goals? Goals will give you a target and lead you to your destination. Goals give you a reason for getting out of bed in the morning. When it comes to goals many of us have never been taught how to actually set them. So, in this chapter I am going to do just that.

What is the difference between a goal and a dream? A lot of us have dreams. We want to take

take over the world, we want to be rich, we want to marry a prince or princess. These are great and these are dreams but they are not goals. Goals have five key elements. We refer to this with the acronym S.M.A.R.T.

Let's start with the first letter S. When it comes to goals be SPECIFIC. You have to get as specific as possible with what it is you want to achieve. Saying that you want to be rich is not a specific goal. Saying that you want to earn $150,000 per year is better, but even more specific would be getting down to the real nitty-gritty and talking about how many dollars per week. If you wanted to earn $150,000 per year then you would know that the math on that per month would be $12,500 and you would be looking at $3,125 per week and then if you worked five days a week that would be $625 a day, now that is specific. So whatever the goal is no matter how big, no matter or how small, you want to be specific as possible.

The M is for MEASURABLE. Having a method of tracking progress for that goal is going to make it measurable. Remember, if it can get measured it gets done. So you want to make sure you are setting measurable goals. The A is for ATTAINABLE. Setting attainable goals of something could be a little bit of a debate, because some people may say $150,000 per year in income is attainable where others say that it is not. If it is attainable in your mind then put it down on paper. If you feel strange about putting it down or when you write it and it seems kind of unrealistic, then maybe you can change it. If you are looking to go to Mars and no one has ever been there before, then maybe I would hold off on that one for a little bit. Attainable is going to be key and having an attainable goal is something that you can really visualize.

The R is for REALISTIC. Earning a million dollars a day when you just finish school, in your first year, is not very realistic. Earning $100 a day on the other hand is. So you want to be as realistic as possible. Remember, this is a career and this is only your first year in this career. You want to be realistic and be looking to measure your goals and increase them as you grow. So start with realistic goals so you do not set yourself up for big disappointments.

Lastly, the T is for TIME. A goal is separated from a dream because it is on a timeline. You have an end target date in mind when you are going to achieve this goal by. You want to make sure you are putting a timestamp on the goal, every goal, not just one. All of them need to have a time stamp on them. Remember though, stay realistic. If you want to lose 100 pounds I wouldn't put a timestamp on it for 30 days without almost killing yourself. It is pretty much going to be an impossible goal. Remember to celebrate the big wins, but do not forget about small wins as well. When I look at someone's success rate, the way that I look at it is, as long as you are taking one small step towards your goal every single day you are successful. One of the other important parts about goal setting is visualizing. I remember someone telling me that they wanted to get a certain car I asked him why he wanted to get it. He said because he really liked it. We turned this into a goal and got really specific. We narrowed down the model, narrowed down the actual color, the exterior and interior. Once we got the specifics we were able to visualize the car. The visualization process led me to find out that he had never driven this car or even seen it. I told him that I wanted him to do me a favor. I wanted him to set a date, go to the dealership, and test drive this car. Getting this specific is what will give you the power of visualization, because now not only do you see the car being yours, you feel it. You can feel the motor running when you are behind the wheel. You feel the grip of the steering wheel in your hands. You feel the seats underneath you and when you are looking out the windshield you start to take ownership. Visualization is going to be key. You have to see yourself there first. If it is losing weight, making money, or buying that dream house, I want you to visualize.

One if the activities that I do with my team,

which is my favorite part of the beginning of every year, is a goal setting workshop. We actually create vision boards and dream boards. We look through magazines and cut out pictures of the dream house, the dream car, the dream vacation spot, and through this process, once we put our pictures on a poster board, we create a vision board or dream board. This is a great way to visualize your dreams. One of the other important aspects of goal setting is, having an accountability partner. Who are you going to be accountable to and who is going to be measuring your progress? If you do not have an accountability partner the likelihood of you hitting any of your goals is slim to none. You should be talking with your accountability partner on a regular basis. Daily would be best, but at least weekly. You definitely do not want to go longer than a month in between talks. Your accountability partner is there to remind you and ask you how you are doing and see what your progress is.

Looking at the increments that you set goals in is another key step. I like to set goals in 30, 60, and 90 day ranges. So that would give you short term, medium and long-term goals. Even though 90 days does not seem that long, if you think about it right now, what are you going to be doing in three months? Many people cannot even see past the next day! Being able to visualize the 30, 60 and 90 day increments will give you different ranges and different goals to be working towards.

Sharing your goals is also very important. Think about who you would want to share your goals with. You definitely want to share your goals with anyone that is going to support you in achieving them. You do not want to share your goals with someone that is going to make fun of them or someone that you are competing against. Someone you are up against for a promotion or you are trying to move into a position that they obtain. You definitely do not want to share that goal with them because you will not get any support. Sharing your goals is going to be key.

One of the diagrams that I am including is going to be a goal wheel. It is divided into the five key areas of goal setting, starting with physical goals. Maybe it is to gain weight or to lose weight. This will apply to any physical attribute you may want to change. Next is personal goals or personal achievements that you want to gain. Next Business and financial goals. Where do you want to see your business go in the next 30 days, 60 days, and 90 days? Where do you want to see your finances? There are also Professional goals. As a professional stylist, where do you want to see your professional skill set? Be it in the next 30, 60, and 90 days. Then there are your Spiritual goals. Maybe you are religious, maybe not, but having a sense of who you are and being in touch with yourself is going to be a key part of your spiritual being. These are the five major areas for goal setting. I recommend having at least a short, medium, and long range goal for each of these areas. You can use the goal setting wheel to set those goals.

There are going to be a few things you want ask when you are setting your goals. Think about creating a long range list. As you begin this process I want you to try to fast forward 10 years and list out 50 things that you want to have happen in your life during this time. Just put on some music and hit the pen to the paper and start writing. Once you go through this and have your fifty things on paper start classifying them into short, medium, and long. As you go through the process you have to think about what makes sense to focus on first. Once you have all of your short, medium and long range goals, you are going to want to focus on the shortlist for next year. You will start working inside of that list and do the same thing. Look at short, medium, and long range goals. This is going to help narrow your goals down to what should be your immediate focus. Having that big picture thinking is great for your imagination and it stimulates possibilities of what you can achieve. You really need to push hard to get down as many goals as possible.

The next step you are going to do is write a

paragraph. Once you narrow down your top five goals in a short range form, you want to write a paragraph as to why they are important to you. This is really going to require you to talk to yourself and you either are going to do two things. You are going to talk yourself into it or you can talk yourself out of it. So make sure you are in a good place you have no distractions while you do this exercise.

When it comes to setting your goals remember your 'why'. As your 'why' gets stronger and bigger, achieving your goals gets a lot easier. A few other questions I want you to ask yourself. What kind of person will it take to get all that you want? When you think about what the person looks like, I want you to write a paragraph describing that person in detail and remember the major value in setting goals is to entice you to become that person. You are going to become the person it takes to achieve them. Goals are something you attract not something you pursue.

Lastly, you have your major goals in all different key areas and you know the type of person that you are going to need to become to achieve those goals. I am going to leave you with some final steps. Write a letter to yourself from the future. Date the letter and write, "Dear self". As you start to write this, I want you to write it in a story format as having already achieved those goals. For example, "Dear Sonny, It is

December 31, 2017. What an incredible year it has been. I have achieved..." and then you will start to go into what you have achieved personally, professionally, physically, spiritually, financially, and business. Keep this letter in a place that you can read it every single day. I recommend having several copies and one of those copies you may even want to laminate it so you can have it in a place like your bathroom and if it gets wet it will not be ruined. Does this sound like a little bit too much? Well, just to give you an example of the power of goal setting I want to share with you a quick story. In 1952 the graduating class of Yale University did a study of the graduating seniors. There were only 10% of them who had goals that were well-defined and written down. Over 30 years they tracked the graduating class. Of that graduating class the 10% that had written down, well-defined goals had achieved more than the other 90% combined. Goal setting is not a myth. Goal setting is not a theory. Goal setting works, it is a fact. When you are setting goals there are a couple rules of thumb. You never want to reduce your target. You may need to extend the timeline, but you never ever want to reduce the target. Remember, these are your goals. They are not anyone else's. It is not up to the salon owner that you work for. It is not up to a spouse, a relative or friend to make you or force you to achieve them. You will have an accountability partner, but ultimately it is going to rely on you to stay focused on your goals and keep them in front of you at all times. When you are going through a rough patch or you going through a trial or tribulation, which I guarantee will happen along your journey, this is when your goals are going to be critical. Reading your goal statement will connect you back to the reason why you decided to go on this journey in the first place. It will connect you back to your why and it will help guide you through. Make sure you are updating your goal statement on a regular basis. At least quarterly so you can look and measure goals you have achieved and take off and replace with new ones. You do not want to be that person that sets goals for their New Year's resolution and by January 15 has already given up on them. Set goals using this format and set goals seriously. Set goals smart and you will achieve them.

Although you may have many goals in all areas of your life you can use the Major Goal setting wheel to list your 3 major goals in each of the 5 key goal setting areas. This tool is great to visualize your complete goal setting picture. Post this somewhere so that you'll be able to see it daily along with your written goal statement.

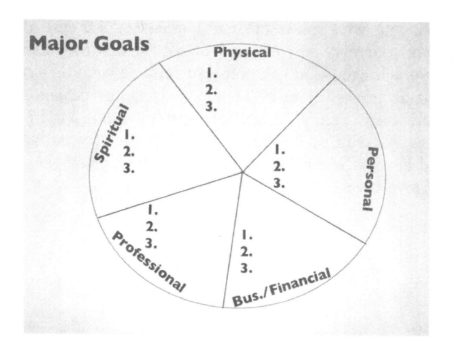

Major Goal Wheel

CHAPTER 8

*Preparation is key. Life seemingly does
not wish to waste success on the
unprepared. ~ Unknown*

Mentors vs. Coaches - Why You
Need Them Both

A lot of us have mentors and some of us have coaches. Typically, when you think about a coach you think about when you were playing in a little league or cheerleading or you were doing some kind of organized activity when you were in school. As an adult, professional coaches are still critical to your success. What is the difference between mentors and coaches? Mentors are people that you can be inspired by or you can look up to. You may or may not have a personal relationship or ever meet them, but looking at what they have done and accomplished is something that you may model or aspire to be. A coach, on the other hand, is someone who will actually work with you and is going to coach you along the way to get you where you want to go. Coaches are going tell you when you are doing right and they are also going to tell you when you need to "take a lap". You need to have both. I have had many different coaches and I have had several mentors throughout my career. I do know I would not be where I am today without either of them. So in this chapter I am going to share with you some of my mentors and how I view mentoring and coaching.

When you are looking for a mentor they are easy to find. They are all over the place. One of my favorites, for example, is Steve Jobs. The incredible thing about Steve Jobs is that he revolutionized and changed the thinking of an entire industry which in effect changed the world. He was bold. He was a visionary. He was a thinker and he had the nerve to tell everyone that was making cellphones to get rid of their buttons and think differently and they all did it. He built an incredible business and even though he was let go from the company that he started, when the company was desperate and almost on the brink of bankruptcy, they brought him back. He turned it around and turn it in to the juggernaut that Apple is today. He is an incredible mentor.

Martin Luther King is another incredible

mentor of mine. His conviction and belief in his product, which was not even tangible, only something that existed in the minds of men and women. It was a dream, but his conviction and his dedication is one of the reasons why he is one of my mentors. Having a vision and having belief are going to be key ingredients when you are looking for mentors.

The creator of Facebook, Mark Zuckerberg, at 30 years old he has incredible vision and incredible focus to be able to have accomplished what he has done so far. As of this writing, Facebook has made Mark Zuckerberg worth over $30 billion and he has become one of the youngest billionaires in the history of man kind. One of his famous quotes that inspires me every time I read it is, this one, "I'm here to build something for the long term. Anything else is a distraction." To have that kind of focus at such a young age when he started and still have it today is very inspiring to me. As you are looking at building your business you need to be able to harness focus and stick with it. You must not get distracted. Your first year, especially, is going to be critical to your success and to focus is mandatory. Next is John Paul Dejoria and Paul Mitchell, the cofounders of John PaulMitchell systems. The two of them, starting with just a vision and $700, have built John Paul Mitchell Systems into what it is today. With over 30 years of success, to think of their beginnings and to where they are now, is very inspiring. In the face of homelessness and a rejection from the majority of the first people that they approached, they kept on working and they never ever gave up. Even though Paul Mitchell passed away over 20 years ago John Paul continues to be not only a mentor of mine but someone that I have had the pleasure to meet and speak with on several occasions. He is someone I truly admire as a leader, as a visionary, and as an entrepreneur.

Another mentor and coach is Robert Cromeans. This one is personal for me because of Roberts impact on me. Just over 10 years ago the course of my life change forever and it was because of him. He is not only a mentor as a business owner, leader and a visionary, but also he is a coach. I have been able to learn from him personally on different ways to grow my business and advance my career. In just a few minutes, if you spend time with him you will know exactly what I mean. His view of the beauty industry and the way that he looks at business is unique and unparalleled to anyone else. Now what about coaches? One of my favorite coaches of all time is Phil Jackson. When it comes to coaching I do not think there is any other one that can match what he has been able to accomplish. Not only 11 rings, 11 championship rings in the NBA, but also the players that he has been able to develop. He had the privilege of coaching the best basketball player arguably on the planet, Michael Jordan. He also had the challenge of assembling players into a championship team with different characters. One of those characters was Dennis Rodman who proved in his time during the NBA to be one of the most uncoachable players. Phil Jackson was able to harness Dennis Rodman's talent and turn that energy and that wild charisma into a championship player. The amazing thing is that Phil Jackson did this not only once, but he did it again and this time it was coaching the Los Angeles Lakers. He had a young Kobe Bryant and Shaquille O'Neal and through his coaching ability, leadership skills, and influence he was able to pull together those two dynamic players and turn them into championship players.

So, as you are looking at the beauty industry you are going to need a nice combination of not only mentors, but also coaches. One of the things that I recommend is that you begin the process of tracking down your mentors, make it a habit, make it a practice, and learn as much as you can about them. Through this you will be learning an important process of developing yourself as a professional called modeling. Modeling your mentors is something I would highly recommend. Keeping a list, doing the research, and looking for any opportunity that you would ever have to meet your mentors. One of the things I've practiced over the years is having a board of advisors.

My board of advisors consist of all the people that I just mentioned to you and a few more. Now those advisers do not even know that they are on my board, but as I go through my career or have decisions I have to make I use my board of advisors. I use them as a sounding board. Having read their biographies, any books and materials, and studied them over the years, I try to think of any challenges or problems that I have and present it to them and see how they would handle it. This may sound a little bit crazy, but this is one of the secrets of the successful. You are also going to want to look at different mentors for different areas of your life. You may have different mentors when it comes to business and finance versus professional. You will have different mentors when it comes to personal versus physical. You can have as many mentors as you want. The important thing is that you have mentors.

When it comes to a coach, having one is going to be critical on your road to success. When you arrive at the salon that you are looking to work at you want to know what kind of coaching opportunities are going to exist. How often are you going to be able to meet and get coaching and feedback. Whoever you are reporting to, whether it be the salon owner or the salon manager, in order to become a professional and become an all-star player you are going to need coaching. As your career progresses look at seeking outside coaching. One of my coaches I talk to twice a month just over the phone and they help hold me accountable and go through my goals, my plans, and my activities. Having a coach helps keep me on track, helps keep me focused, keeps my head in the game, and helps keep my eyes on the target. So you ultimately need to have both. You want to have coaches and you want to have mentors. This is one thing that I know as I was making my way into the beauty industry that I would have been lost without. Being able to have mentors to look up to, books and audio programs about their mistakes, discoveries, and their path along the way, has helped me tremendously through the years and I know it will do the same for you. I highly advise you start building your board of advisors today.

CHAPTER 9

If you're not satisfied with your environment, answer this question. Have you committed 100%? If not then your environment probably hasn't either. ~ Sonny D

Location-Location-Location - Why bouncing around will ruin your career

Ok so you finally decided to start working. You found the right salon and you are ready to begin the journey. As you begin the journey you discover along the way maybe this is not the place for you so then you start looking around for a new opportunity. A friend tells you about another salon that just opened up. So you go have an interview and start working at your second salon. After a while you decide there may be another opportunity and this starts the path that will slowly, but surely, ruin your career. As you are beginning you need to think building your career will be just like building a house. First you will need to find a plot of land to do all the excavation and make sure that everything looks good so you can begin to build. As you start laying the foundation if you see another plot of land and go over there, what do you think is going to happen? You are not going pick up where you left off, you are going to have to start building all over again. Before you know it, you have all these little foundations that you started building, time is going by, months turn into years, and years turn into nothing. Bouncing around from one location to another location, I have seen cause a very slow death to many stylists careers. Using the interviewing tips that I shared earlier, you want to make sure that when you are going to commit to a salon that you plan to stay there and build. You are going to be building goodwill not only between yourself and the salon owner, but between yourself and the guest. When you think that you are going leave and all of your guests that you have been working with are going to follow you, you are sorely mistaken. Will some guess follow you? Sure they will, but typically what we see is when somebody leaves they lose roughly 70 to 80% of their business. If you do that one or two times you are completely starting from scratch. I worked in a salon where I had guest tell me they did not know what they would do if I left. They said if I ever left they would be lost without me. The reality is when the time came and I did leave to start my own business those guests were nowhere to be found. That is the reality of guest loyalty. You have to remember this is a business. Those guests are loyal to the location that they are going to and once you have created a pattern for them and they are used to going to that location that is most likely what they are going to remain doing. So when you are deciding on a salon I want you to think about not going to work for the commission, but going to work for the salon. What do I mean by that? I will share a short story with you.

There were two guys Dave and Bill that went to work for a railroad. They started working the same day and they began doing the same job. One day Dave was out there in the hot sun pounding away as a railroad car slowly started to approach. The railroad car came to a stop and someone leaned out the window and yells, "Dave! Dave Anderson!" Dave wipes sweat from his brow and looks up and noticed it was his friend Bill. He went over to the car and they embraced. Bill invited him inside and they sat and talked for what seemed to be maybe an hour. They embraced once more and Dave went back out to work. As he walked back out into the hot sun over to the crew one of the guys said to Dave, "Hey Dave is that Bill? Bill Murphy, the president of the railroad?"

"Yup, it sure is. We have been friends for over 20 years. 20 years ago we started at this railroad on the same day."

The coworker asked, "How is it that you are still out here working in the hot sun and Bill Murphy is the president of the railroad?" Dave, without hesitation, said, "It is pretty simple. 20 years ago when we started this job I went to work for five dollars an hour. Bill, on the other hand, he went to work for the railroad."

The moral of the story is, when you decide to go to a salon you decide to join that salon. You decide to go to work for that salon, not for the commission, not for the paycheck. That is how you are going to build goodwill. That is how you are going build a solid business.

The opportunity may come for you to travel and you do not have to limit yourself to the city or state that you live in. When you are looking for an ideal position in the salon be open-minded. Use tools available to you to see what else is available out there. I recommend to interview at least three salons before you make a decision. Look at the pros and cons and use the salon interview tips that I shared in an earlier chapter. Make a decision and once you make it you need to think about sticking to it.

Location is important. In some cases, though, you may find a location that is not on a busy main street, but may have all of the other attributes that you are looking for. So you want to weigh those against each other. If you are depending on only the salon location to bring in clientele you need to go back and read the networking chapter. I have salons that are in prime locations and I have salons that experience a high-volume of walk-in traffic. Some experience a lower volume of walk-in traffic, but the difference maker for any stylist will always comes down to that stylist. So you want to consider that traffic is not the only deciding factor. You also want to consider when you are working in the location that you are farming around that location. You want to make yourself a frequent patron in different places around that location. Your first year in the beauty industry is really going to be your hardest year, so just remember that it does take time. If you are coming into an established salon, you may have that support from the salon to receive new guests that are coming in, but I would not rely on that solely. Making a firm commitment to the location that you are at is the quickest way to build your business. One of my stylist that I can think of that has been with our company for six years has a former classmate ,that for the same amount of time, has continued to bounce around from salon to salon to salon. As I watch this individual still continue to struggle, it seems like every year they are rebuilding their clientele. Meanwhile the stylist of my salon has experienced 10 times the growth in the same amount of time.

Not by coincidence, it is by commitment. Commit to a location, commit to a salon, stay put, and you will build a solid business that continues to pay you for the years to come. As I like to say "Stick and stay is bound to pay!"

CHAPTER 10

If you've got a problem man or money can solve you ain't got no problem. ~ T.D. Jakes

What if you do make it?

So we are coming in for a landing. You are on your way and going to make it through your first year in the beauty industry. You are not going to be a part of the statistics, but what happens now? I do not want you to let your guard down and think that it is going to be smooth sailing from here on out. The first year is the hardest year in the beauty industry so I do want to congratulate you on accomplishing that, but I do want you to also know that the journey really has just begun. In this first year, using a lot of the tips and strategies that I have shared, hopefully you have been able to land in the right salon, build a solid clientele, have more confidence, and have a good handle on your business.

So what is next? This is a career so I need to be thinking about it like this, building a solid career is a time intensive process. It is like running a marathon. It is not a sprint. It is not a 100 yard dash. You are going to continue repeating the process and using the tips and strategies that I shared every single year while you are continuing to build. If you look at building your career as kind of like a project that never ends. Look at it like that, but eventually you will get to a point where you are ready to retire.

There are just a couple of tips I want to share and some pitfalls I see new stylist coming into the industry make that maybe I can help you avoid. You want to be future minded. You want to be planning. Now depending on if you are working for commission or if you are working for hourly pay, you may be responsible for your own taxes. I am not an accountant nor financial advisor, but I will tell you this, I have seen 1099 independent contractors not prepare properly for taxes. By not saving a portion of their paycheck, at least 15%, end up with some pretty serious tax bills that they are unable to pay. You do not want to end up in this predicament so I want you to be thinking about future planning and get in touch with a CPA and financial planner to set up your strategy.

One of the other things I see happen is some

stylists start to have some financial success when they make it through their first year and they start to earn more so therefor they spend more. That is just human nature. I do not think it is anything unique to just stylists, I just think it is the way people are. I am going to recommend that you live off less than you make. Try to live off of 70% of your money. The other 30% you can use to save, invest, and maybe give back. That formula seems to work and is just a rule of thumb, but definitely living off less than you make is a good strategy. I have seen stylists start to earn money, overextend their credit, over overextend boundaries, then end up in a position that forces them to make bad decisions. Do not let that happen to you. As you are looking ahead know that the future is coming. Just because you may not be able to see it, it will be here. So if you start the plan for your future now you will be able to reap the rewards when it comes.

When it comes to pricing some stylist, if they're independent, may have their own strategy. Know this, if you are working in the salon or if you have your own ability to set your prices, through continuing training and education you should be looking to be promoted. How often you are promoted depends. I have seen some stylist charge the same price year after year after year and wonder why they are not making any money or things still seem tight. You have to think about it like this, inflation is real. Prices go up on goods and services every year so it should be no different for you. You are a professional providing professional services and as long as you are continuing to train and educate yourself you are entitled to an increase in earnings just like anybody else. If you are working in a salon and the salon owner has a career path in place then you will be able to use that to your advantage. Know how it works and know how you can continue to raise your level of income. Your future really depends on you. When you decided to go to beauty school and decided to join the beauty industry, you decided to join an industry where there is potential for you to enjoy an amazing career with enormous financial benefits, as well as doing satisfying work that brings joy to many people. You have to keep in mind that this is a business and this is a career and just because you made it through your first year you do not want to rest on your laurels or let your guard down. You want to continue to grow and continue to build.

Here are a couple of other suggestions. Now that you made it how do you pay it forward? When you look at the stylist that are coming up, you should take it upon yourself to offer any advice or tips that you learned along the way. Maybe that means you go back to your beauty school and donate some of your time as a guest artist to share your knowledge. That will be reassuring and inspiring for people that are coming up in the industry. Remember that the people that are coming up after you have the same kind of fears, doubts, and frustrations as you did. They need information and seeing someone that is making it and comes back and shares not only will help them, but is also very rewarding for yourself. So pay it forward by offering to do things like that.

So where to next? The journey has just begun and you made it through the toughest part. Seeing so many people quit just before they reach that level of success really upsets me. If there was a way that I could fast forward and show them the potential and the opportunity then I definitely would do it. I guess this is my way. To be able to share with you things that I have learned and seen in stylist that I have worked with as well as my own career, maybe this gives you a glimpse into the future. The first years are extremely hard, but if you build your business the right way and you approach this as a career you will be able to take advantage of the compounding effects.

I want to give you a quick overview of the miracle of compounding. Albert Einstein actually refers to compounding as the eighth wonder of the world. If you were to take a penny and you were to double it for 30 days do you think you would be able to come up with any serious money at the end? A lot of times when I use this example I offer a person a penny the doubles every day for thirty days or one million dollars. Many people take the million dollars because they want instant gratification. I guess that is the world we live in, but if you think about it, a penny doubling every day for the next 30 days takes advantage of the miracle of compounding. In the beginning just like your career it does not seem like much. Even after the first week or the first two weeks, you start to wonder if you took the wrong option because by day seven you only have $0.64 and by day 14 you only have $81.92. The magic of compounding takes time. Just like building your career. You are not going to be rich after the first 12 months and probably not after the first 24 months, but with the power of compounding, the penny, by day number 24 you are up to $83,000 and by day number 25 you are up to $167,000. The real miracle does not kick in until day 27. In the days that follow up to that, up to day 31, you go from $671,000 on day 27 to $10,700,000 on day 31. That million dollars today does not seem so impressive now does it? So what it's going to take for you is to have patience, to be persistent, and to be consistent. That is how you are going to build a career. Making it through the first year is hard, but it does get easier. If you keep focused and keep working it you will be able to take advantage of the same effects. I have seen it happen in my own career and I have also been able to coach stylist in and outside of my company and see it happen for them. Unfortunately, for the ones who leave and do not make it through their first year they will never know the true beauty of this industry. So I hope this book is able to help you and if so please let me know about your success along the way. I wish you the most incredible journey and the most the incredible career that you deserve. I cannot wait to see you in the future as a successful, beauty industry professional. **Keep growing!**

FINAL THOUGHTS

So here we are at the end or the beginning depends how you look at it. One thing is for sure if you take and apply what we've talked about the ride is much more enjoyable. Just think, if you stay in the beauty industry for the next say 20 years what do you want those 20 years to look like? This is the time you are setting your foundation and it's crucial that you do it right or you'll do it over. One thing I tell my team all the time is that if I had to start over, with YFYI in my hands, I wouldn't be that afraid. I've done my best to give you the information now it's up to you to apply. Remember

INFORMATION+<u>APPLICATION</u>= TRANSFORMATION

I hope you'll share your journey with me. I can't wait to see you out in the industry doing incredible things!

These are all stories of real people and real numbers. Average age 25. Average time in the beauty industry 3 years. Hopefully one day I'll be writing one on you.

———

———

CASE STUDY #1

———

———

the Devin

Meet Devin or as we like to call him DJ. He's a graduate of Paul Mitchell the school Orlando class of February 2012. He joined our team in August of 2012. He's one of the most sought after men's groomers in the Tampa Bay area. Since joining our team he's done $298,962.29 in services/retail and is on track to do $120,000 in 2015 alone. He operates on an avg. ticket of $63.55 with 5,220 guest visits. In addition to that he's a member of our leadership team which helps develop new talent and carry out the vision of the salon 1.0 follow him @devindoeshair

CASE STUDY #2

the Katrina

Meet Katrina or as we like to refer to her as Katsawz. She's a graduate of Paul Mitchell the school Tampa class of July 2013. She joined team 1.0 in December 2013. Since joining our team she's done $67,839.34 in services/retail and is on track to do $90,000 in 2015. Pretty good for her first full year on the floor huh? She's done that on an avg. ticket of $56.86 and with 1,235 guest visits. She's an example of whats possible if you plug into a system. Keep an eye on this young star. Follow her @katrinasawaska

CASE STUDY #3

the Jenna

Meet Jenna or as we like to refer to her as @jennawasag. She's a graduate of Paul Mitchell the school Tampa class of November 2009. She joined team 1.0 in December 2009 as one of our very first hires. Since joining our team she's done $444,006.85 in services/retail and is on track to do $100,000 plus in 2015. She's done that on an avg. ticket of $67.19 and with 6,723 guest visits. She's also become our first partner/owner in the company and has a major role in company operations. Follow her as she helps lead the future direction of the company. @jennawasag

ACKNOWLEDGMENTS

There's so many people I would like to thank that I'm probably going to need to write another book just for that. But here's a few in particular that influenced this piece of work.

First and foremost my team 1.0 who give me the belief everyday of what's possible, not only in YFYI but beyond. You guys keeps me moving, thank you!

John Paul Dejoria and Winn Claybaugh who without the creation of Paul Mitchell the school you wouldn't be reading this. Thank you for all you have done not only for me but the entire beauty industry. Especially for giving me the belief that no matter where you come from anything is possible.

Stephanie Kocielski and Angus Mitchell for believing in me and believing in second chances. I won't let you down.

Mikel Sandoval, Kevin Michaels, and Giulio Veglio for hiring me for my first two jobs out of beauty school. Also for giving me the mentorship and opportunity to grow even beyond where I thought I could. Tara Dowdal for pulling me out of the financial aid office my first day of school, before I walked out, because I knew I couldn't afford it.

My main man Robert Cromeans, who's to blame for this whole thing getting started. Thanks for guiding me to a Paul Mitchell the school. Thanks for taking me under your wing whether you liked it or I just forced my way under there. Thanks for getting me to see the "big picture" and realize that I am not only building a business but have the opportunity to change the industry or as you once told me "dye trying". Thanks in advance for the job as well, (wink wink). Thank you to Mary for picking me at that model call 10 years ago or I never would have met you all.

Last but certainly not least my business partner, top stylist, but most of all best friend Jenna. Who's been with me through thick and thin. Who without, this book would have never gotten finished. Even though I drive you crazy, sometimes beyond what you signed up for, thanks for believing in me. I love you.

There are many more of you out there I'm sure. THANK YOU too. I'll catch you on the next go round' ... I'm just warming up!

YFYI

YOUR FIRST YEAR IN

CPSIA information can be obtained at www.ICGtesting.com
Printed in the USA
LVOW07s2237200116

471605LV00002B/2/P